Building a World Federation

The Key to Resolving Our Global Crises

Sovaida Ma'ani Ewing

Cover design: Reza Mostmand

ISBN 978-0-9909437-0-9

Also available as an e-book
ISBN 978-0-9909437-1-6

Published by the Center for Peace and Global Governance,
Washington, DC.
Printed in the United States.

Dedicated to Ken, whose love ennobles me and without whose help this book would never have seen the light of day, and to my beloved Gigi, who fills my life with joy and light.

CONTENTS

Introduction   **2**

Changing Habits – A Prerequisite for Success   **8**

Building a World Federation   **10**
The Blueprint for an Institutional Infrastructure   *11*
Foundational Principals Are Our Tools   *13*
Lessons from America and Europe   *18*

Where Are We Now?   **28**
The League of Nations   *28*
The United Nations   *29*
The European Union   *30*

World Federation Solves Global Problems   **32**
The Global Financial Crisis   *33*
Destabilizing Behavior by States   *58*
Climate Change And Soaring Energy Demand   *80*

Responding To Skeptics   **110**

**Conclusion – Act Quickly to Avoid Damaging
Consequences**   **113**

Notes and References   **119**

INTRODUCTION

Humanity, viewed as a collective whole, has been slowly but inexorably moving towards increasing integration. It has successively passed through stages of collective growth characterized by ever-widening circles of integration, social cohesion and loyalty starting with the family and progressing in turn to the tribe, city-state and nation. Given our tremendous advances in the areas of communication, transportation and trade that have made us increasingly and inextricably interdependent, it stands to reason that the next unit of overarching loyalty towards which we are moving is loyalty to the world as a unit. The peacefulness of our societies, which in turn determines the extent to which we can focus our energies on civilization-building activities, is largely determined by the degree of our social cohesion. Yet our progress toward peacefulness has always been uneven. Occasionally we have made great strides and produced impressive and peaceful civilizations. At other times we have not only failed to progress but have retrogressed. The overarching result, however, is one of growth in the direction of increasing integration and unity.

If we were to liken humanity's growth to that of an individual, then our current collective state might best be identified with the period of adolescence, with all its turbulence, exploration of boundaries and flirtation with dangerous and potentially disastrous behavior. Looking on the bright side, adolescence presages maturity, a fact that marks the momentous nature of our current experience and that should give us hope that we will emerge from our current seemingly chaotic and self-destructive state and display some of the much-anticipated evidences of maturity. The hope thus engendered can also galvanize us to expend the effort we need to navigate us through this critical period of adolescence in a way that minimizes the damage we do to ourselves. The hallmark of our collective maturity will be arriving at the next inevitable stage in our collective evolution, namely that of recognizing that our first allegiance must be to the human race as a whole. Having achieved this recognition, we will need to take the second step to craft global institutions and collective decision-making processes that reflect our newfound understanding.

Many factors point to the need for and timeliness of this next step: the first is the reality that in all spheres of life—be they economic, financial, environmental, security or health to name but a few—nations and peoples are inextricably interconnected. Our modern systems of communication, transportation, trade and finance ensure that we live in a world in which one nation can no longer isolate itself from the concerns of other nations and claim that it is self-sufficient, because like it or not, it is not so. Our interests are too inextricably interwoven. Events in one part of the world can affect us all. Little did we expect for example, that a massive earthquake off the Tohuku east coast of Japan in March 2011 would set off a chain of events beginning with a 15-meter tsunami that would cause scientists to be concerned about the potential damage to human and biological health along the West Coast of Canada and the United States. Yet, the tsunami knocked out power to cooling pumps at the site of a nuclear power plant in the Fukushima-Daiichi prefecture leading to a partial meltdown of three of the plant's four reactors and the subsequent release of large amounts of radioactive material, particularly cesium, into the waters of the Pacific Ocean. It was the worry triggered by such large releases that led scientists to put in place a program to monitor the coastal waters of North America on a periodic basis.[1]

Another factor is the reality that the gravest problems facing humanity are collective in nature and demand collective solutions. Global warming is a prime example. Caused by the release into the biosphere of excessive amounts of greenhouse gases, chief among them carbon dioxide generated everywhere that fossil and other biological materials are burned for energy, the temperature of the earth's surface is increasing at an historically unprecedented speed and triggering many kinds of damaging effects. These effects include melting glaciers and ice-caps that lead in turn to rising ocean levels that threaten to submerge entire island nations and large swathes of coastal areas around the world. As a result there will be less land to house growing populations and less arable land to feed them. Experts predict that these realities will inevitably lead to conflict over land and resources.

The proliferation of weapons of mass destruction including nuclear, chemical and biological weapons is another example of a global problem that demands a collective solution, inasmuch as it poses a threat to international peace and security. Such proliferation sows the seeds of fear and suspicion among nations leading them to amass arms in an ever-increasing quest to assure their own security. The greater the number of destructive armaments we amass and the higher the degree of fear, the greater are the chances that such weapons will be used deliberately or accidentally. Even if such armaments are ultimately used within a specific locality or region, experience teaches us that their use often has cascading and ever-widening, destabilizing effects on neighboring countries, regions and eventually beyond them to other nations.

The challenge of dealing with the behavior of rogue states that sponsor terrorism or commit genocide or other human rights atrocities on a large scale is yet another example of a global problem that calls for a collective solution. A good example that illustrates the regional and global ramifications of such problems can be seen in the single example of Syria. In a bid to quash internal dissent, the Syrian government began, in March of 2010, to use excessive force including chemical arms against its own people. By doing so, Syria triggered both a civil war and a severe refugee crisis that have resulted in one of the worst humanitarian crises of our times. More than three million Syrians have fled Syria as refugees.[2] Most of them have sought refuge in neighboring countries where their presence is exerting excessive social and economic pressures that, it is feared, may destabilize those countries in turn. For example there are more than one million Syrian refugees in Lebanon alone, a country whose total native population is only 4.5 million. Of these, 830,000 are registered in Turkey and 613,000 in Jordan. In addition to the three million who have fled Syria as refugees, the UN Refugee Agency estimates that a further 6.5 million Syrians are displaced within Syria, which means that half of the Syrian population has had to flee their homes.[3] In addition to the refugee and humanitarian crises, Syria's behavior has also stoked a civil war that has encouraged the growth of internal militias while also providing fertile ground for terrorist networks such as the Islamic State of Iraq and the Levant (otherwise known as "ISIL") to flourish. The increasing influence of ISIL and its wanton acts of violence including mass executions and extrajudicial killings, especially in neighboring Iraq, have in turn triggered a tremendous amount of instability in the region and have caused other countries including Britain, France, Australia, the United States, Saudi Arabia, the UAE, Bahrain and Jordan to intervene to prevent a further deterioration that would affect both their interests and the peace and security of the world.[4]

Even problems that at first blush appear to be limited in their effect to one nation or region can quickly become matters of vital importance to the security of the world at large. Our recent history is replete with examples of rapidly spreading viruses like SARS, bird flu and Ebola that have the potential to become pandemics that threaten the well-being and survival of large numbers of human beings worldwide. The 2014 outbreak of the deadly Ebola virus in West Africa is the most recent example of this. Although initially viewed as a local or regional problem, six months after its outbreak, health officials began to express alarm at its rapid growth. They began to report that the virus was growing exponentially and started describing it as a potential threat to global security that needed to be dealt with swiftly and with force. Indeed, the community of nations concluded that the danger the virus posed to the international community was of such gravity, that it merited being taken up by the UN Security Council as a matter of urgency.[5] Eventually, nations recognized that because of the degree of global interconnectedness, as evidenced by the amount of travel between nations, if a herculean effort was not made to stamp out the virus in West Africa, the scene of this latest outbreak, the virus would spread and threaten the security of people in other continents as well.

There are many other such collective problems. Yet the community of nations lacks the collective decision-making institutions and mechanisms to find collective solutions for these shared global problems. The only viable answer, as yet untried, lies in building a world federation of nations. It is an idea whose time has come. And yet, the multiplicity of global crises facing the world suggests that we are lagging behind in establishing the institutional infrastructure required to support our emerging global society. We can remedy this delay by taking the necessary steps towards establishing such infrastructure in the form of a world federation. If we return to the metaphor of humanity as a collective whole being like an individual going through various stages of growth, we begin to understand why we have so many global problems. Just as an individual who skips or delays a crucial stage in her development will begin to exhibit signs of social retardation, as exemplified for example in the life of the 40-year old who insists on behaving like an 18-year old and is therefore incapable of assuming the responsibilities of a spouse, parent or even reliable employee, so, too, humanity having delayed a crucial step in its collective development, is bound to exhibit signs of collective retardation and manifest collective problems, social, economic and otherwise. Such an understanding may well explain the insatiable and immature desire of consumers and businesses to spend beyond their means, or the sense of entitlement that leads them to believe that they should be entitled to social benefits without having to work too many hours, or their belief that we are entitled to retire early or not pay our share of taxes. It may also explain the unwillingness of our world's leaders to take the difficult decisions necessary to arrest global warming, or to create the international regulations and enforcement mechanisms to ensure that countries do not take on excessive debt, or to take collective action to unseat genocidal leaders from power. Are not all of these omissions evidence of an unwillingness to grow up and change our ways? Such an understanding may also provide us with the incentive we need to work quickly to establish the necessary institutions and to acquire the behaviors and habits that are required for the next stage of our collective development that will hopefully be marked by a true and lasting peace rather than to see our global problems multiply and deepen. We must work tirelessly to identify a viable system for nations of the world to take collective decisions that alleviate world problems and lead to peace and security.

CHANGING HABITS – A PREREQUISITE FOR SUCCESS

At the root of all our seemingly intractable global problems lies an unwillingness to acknowledge that some of our habits, assumptions, attitudes, policies, laws and institutions have not only ceased to serve our best interests or conduce to our happiness, but instead are positively harming us. Yet if we are to make progress and solve our immense global challenges we must change our antiquated ways of being, rather than sacrificing ourselves to maintain them.

One important change is to abandon the habit of expediency, which leads us to make decisions based on narrow and short-term self-interest. This approach to solving global problems may appear to solve the problem at hand in the short-term but usually spawns new problems in the long-term that we have not foreseen because of our short-term focus. For example, training and arming the Mujahedeen to fight the Soviet Army in Afghanistan though successful in dislodging the Soviets from Afghanistan created a new problem for America in the form of the Taliban. America subsequently fought a war to topple the Taliban and has remained mired in the aftermath of that war for many years. It was such a short-term calculation that led governments in certain countries to bow to public pressure after the Fukushima nuclear disaster in Japan and announce that they would close a number of their power-generating nuclear plants and turn instead to dirty fossil fuels, particularly coal, as a substitute source of energy. In doing so, politicians were willing to take actions they knew would exacerbate the risks of global warming, with long-term deleterious consequences for the lives of their own people as well as the rest of the world, simply to cater to their own political short-term interests.

The other problem with expediency is that the solutions crafted in response to various problems often end up being incongruent with each other and actively undermine each other. For example although the international community claimed in the aftermath of the Rwandan genocide that it would never again stand idly by and allow such human rights atrocities to occur, when faced with massive human atrocities committed by agents of the Sudanese government against the people of Darfur starting in 2003, resulting in the death of at least 480,000 individuals and the displacement of over 2 million others, the international community found itself paralyzed yet again. The Security Council, the United Nations agency tasked with maintaining international peace and security, was unable to pass a resolution imposing sanctions on Sudan in a bid to stop the genocide because one of its permanent members, China, having invested heavily to secure Sudanese oil production concessions to help satisfy China's vast and soaring energy demands, threatened to veto any sanctions that would threaten these narrow self-interests.

The habit of expediency is unfortunately one that is currently deeply engrained in the way we conduct international relations. It is time that our world leaders take steps to ensure it gives way to a more constructive habit, that of taking a long-term view of the collective interests of humanity when attempting to solve any given global problem.

BUILDING A WORLD FEDERATION

Having established the correct attitudinal and psychological environment among nations, the question is how do we set about building a world federation? It is apt to consider the following analogy: Whenever we set out to build a new edifice, we begin with a design produced by a competent and creative architect who considers the needs of those who will use the building and the purposes it is intended to serve, as she combines imagination and skill to produce her design. However, a design alone is insufficient: nothing will ever be built if we don't have the proper materials, tools and equipment for the job. Finally, we look to the past experience of seasoned builders for pointers on solving particularly complicated problems, to warn against typical pitfalls, and to encourage us. Applying this analogy as we set about building a global federation of nations, we will be better able to design a federation that will effectively and permanently solve our global challenges. We can draw on the work of thinkers and historical models to help us craft a design that will satisfy our needs. We can also identify and agree upon a set of foundational principles of international relations that we can uncompromisingly use as tools to implement our design. The materials we work with are the factual circumstances surrounding any given global problem. The American experience of forging a federated state applying certain principles of federalism can also serve as a useful guide. This, in short, constitutes a complete formula for action. We will examine each element of the formula in turn.

The Blueprint for an Institutional Infrastructure

The infrastructure of a world federal government should encompass at least some important institutions.

World Legislature

The first of these is a world legislature, the members of which are elected by the people of each country and confirmed by their respective governments. The legislature will enact such laws as are necessary to regulate the relationships of all peoples and nations and address their common challenges and needs. One can imagine that such laws might include a modicum of financial regulation to protect us from the types of financial crises to which we have become prone. They might also include regulation of the kinds and amounts of energy we use to ensure that we do not continue to pollute our environment and create problems like global warming that threaten us with disaster. They are also likely to include food and water regulation to ensure that everyone has fair access to sufficient clean water and healthful food. In addition such laws would include rules on arms production and proliferation as well as rules determining those circumstances in which the federal government can use force to uphold or maintain peace.

Upon this legislature will devolve certain rights that have hitherto been vested in states, which they will willingly cede. They include all rights to maintain arms except in the amount necessary to maintain internal order within national borders, as well as all claims to make war, subject to the principle that the global legislature will sanction the use of force only collectively and in service of justice. The nations will also cede to the legislature certain rights to impose taxes, affording the global legislature the funds to uplift and better the condition of humanity. It is easy to imagine that such funds would be used to find ways of reversing or ameliorating global warming or to find clean renewable sources of energy or to create an international standing army to preserve peace in the world. The nations will also grant to the global legislature complete and exclusive authority over the earth's resources in its capacity as the trustee of the whole of humanity, including many resources that may as yet be undiscovered and untapped, all of which it will tap and fully utilize for the collective interest of humanity. It will also do its utmost to exploit all the available sources of energy. To achieve all of this it will harness the enormous political and economic energy hitherto wasted on war. It will also organize all the economic resources of the world, coordinating and developing the global markets and ensuring that the distribution of products is equitably regulated.

International Court

Another important institution is an international court, essentially a supreme court for the world that will have the authority to adjudicate all disputes arising between nations and all the elements comprising the federal government. In discharging this power it will have compulsory jurisdiction in all cases that threaten the peace, even if parties to a case do not voluntarily agree to submit to its jurisdiction, and its verdicts will be binding and enforceable.

World Executive

A World Executive is another important institution within the ambit of a world federal government. The Executive will have the authority to enforce both international laws enacted by the legislature and decisions of the International Court and generally to deal with any breaches of the peace, thereby safeguarding the organic unity of the world superstate. To achieve these purposes, it will have at its disposal a Standing Army that is made up of the combined forces of the federated units and is therefore representative of all the nations. This Army will act in the collective interests of humanity to preserve the peace and enforce international laws and the judgments of the International Court. Its actions will be subject to the direction of the World Executive, which itself will act according to rules of law to which all have agreed in advance.

Foundational Principals Are Our Tools

To build a world federation we must apply a set of foundational principles without compromise. First we must identify these principles and then build consensus among nations around them along with a commitment to applying them uncompromisingly. Once these steps have been taken we can begin to apply these principles as we would tools for a physical structure, to craft our global federal institutions. This three-step approach is, unfortunately, not one that nations have been accustomed to following. Its importance was stressed by the governing body of the Baha'is in a document it released in 1985 addressed to the people of the world. In this document the following observation was made: "Leaders of government and all in authority would be well served in their efforts to solve problems if they would first seek to identify the principles involved and then be guided by them."[6] Since then other great thinkers of our time have arrived at the same conclusion. One of these thinkers, who served as Foreign Minister of his country as well as on several high-level international commissions and as director of one of the world's most prestigious non-governmental organizations in the field of conflict resolution said, "There is no substitute for going back to first principles, getting consensus around them and then applying them."[7]

What, then, are these foundational principles that might serve as our tools to build a world federation?

Oneness

Probably the most important of all these foundational principles is the principle of the oneness of humanity. All human beings are created noble and equal regardless of the color of their skin, their gender, their nationality or the amount of wealth or education they possess. We are all animated by the same spirit that engenders within us similar hopes, fears and capabilities. We share the same basic hopes and dreams that include living a life in which our basic needs are met, in which our children are educated, healthy and safe and in which we all create meaning by contributing to an ever-advancing civilization. We also share the same fears of want, suffering and a life devoid of meaning. Upon reflection, it appears that most of the problems of our time are attributable to a lack of awareness of this important principle.[8] Once our leaders have deeply grasped this fundamental principle of oneness and have made it the operating principle of international relations, we will we be able to craft collective decision-making institutions that truly represent humanity and give each nation and people a voice, while enabling speedy and effective resolution of problems. The principle of oneness is the foundational tool in building a world federation as it goes to the heart of the essential relationships that bind nations and people together as members of one human family.

Principle of Equality

The principle that nations are to be treated equally is an outgrowth of the principle of oneness. Applying this principle when building a world federation demands, as a prerequisite, that all nations have attained their independence, in the sense that they are not involuntarily colonized by others or subject to modes of government, such as totalitarian regimes, that deny their people fundamental freedoms including the freedom of assembly, expression and belief. The experience of the United States serves as a valuable guide: just as the U.S. Constitution provides for all states to be equally autonomous, so, too, the nations of the world must enjoy equal status within the ambit of a world federation. The principle of equality also implies that nations must be fairly represented within a federal government. Indeed, fairness and justice dictate that no group or nation be given a greater vote or a greater say in collective decisions putting them in a position to dominate others, simply because they believe they are superior, rather than on the basis of a rational and collectively agreed-upon system of fair representation

Working for the Collective Interest

Another powerful principle is that the advantage of the part is best reached by ensuring the advantage of the whole and that there can be no long-term benefit for a component part if the interests of the whole are neglected. In other words, the only way a nation can assure its own self-interest is by working assiduously for the collective interest of all nations. This was the lesson that the countries of Western Europe learned in the aftermath of the Second World War. Decimated and crushed as their infrastructure, economies and societies were, the countries of Europe all sought coal and steel on equal terms to rebuild themselves. They also wanted to ensure that advantageous access to coal and steel did not allow Germany to initiate another war. The solution they ultimately agreed upon was to pool their coal and steel resources under the management of a supranational High Authority that was given expansive powers to ensure that each member country had access to the coal and steel it needed on fair terms and that all production and sales of these materials were transparent to all. The common market for coal and steel that was thus born was known as the European Coal and Steel Community (ECSC). Significantly, the nations that formed this new European Coal and Steel Community joined only after long debate and analysis led each to conclude, in its particular political, economic, and historical situation, that its interests would be served better by acting together with other nations for the collective interest of all the members, than by going it alone. It is also significant that, having understood this fundamental principle, each of the six founding member nations willingly gave up some sovereignty over these two critical resources — the functional equivalents of oil and gas for us today — to a supranational agency working for the collective interests of all. Most significantly, the creation of an institution based on the principle of the need to work for the collective advantage (as well as other principles identified above) brought peace to Europe after centuries of intermittent wars and was the first step in the gradual evolution of what we know today as the European Union, a union that currently embraces twenty-eight European states within its ambit.

Limit National Sovereignty While Avoiding Excessive Centralization

A principle that is closely allied with, and an outgrowth of, the principle that nations must work in the collective interest of all is the need to limit national sovereignty. This principle demands that all national impulses be subordinated to the requirements of a unified world. Although this principle requires that all nations be willing to cede control over certain important powers they possess, in areas where collective action serves their interests better than individual action, it does not aim to do away with nation states. Rather it recognizes that these states serve a useful function as distinct identifiable entities responsible for the welfare and protection of their people, and accountable to them and to the international community for any failure to discharge this weighty responsibility. Nor does it aim to snuff out the kind of intelligent patriotism that motivates citizens of each country to contribute to the advancement of the arts, sciences, education, health and general welfare of their country, nor does it seek to impose a unity based on uniformity. On the contrary, it is important that nation states continue to exercise authority and power in certain domains to avoid the dangers of excessive centralization on the one hand while also encouraging and maintaining diversity within the context of a unified federation of states.

Other Tools

The principles identified above are the most fundamental and powerful ones in building a world federation. However, there are others including the principle that force may only be used in the service of justice and for the larger good, according to rules agreed by all nations in the federation. Humanity does not appear to have reached a point in its evolution in which it can do away with the use of force altogether. Its use must, however, be severely limited and regulated. It must be used only after a collective decision is made by institutions representing all the nations and people of the world based on collectively-agreed rules and by a force that represents all the nations of the world. Under this system, all nations must limit the amounts of their arms to the minimum required to preserve peace and order within their borders. Any additional arms must be destroyed. Moreover, they must also agree that if a nation breaches the terms of the international agreement on peace and security, all the nations of the world will arise to bring down that government and replace it with one that can work as a peaceful member of the community of nations. To achieve this, the community of nations must have an international Standing Army at its disposal.

Lessons from America and Europe

Once leaders of nations have agreed both on the blueprint for a world federation and the foundational principles to be applied in building it, they will find that the American experience of building a federated nation and the continuing European experiment of deepening integration can provide valuable lessons of what to do and what to avoid along the way.

The American Experience

Several aspects of the American experience of moving from a divided community of diverse and loosely related states to a federation deserve closer examination as we move down the path to a world federation. In the days preceding the union, the former colonies were rife with skepticism about the possibility of creating an American federa-

18

tion. Many believed that insuperable barriers stood in the way of such an achievement. This view was based on the argument that there were too many conflicting interests in play, too much distrust, and too many differences, both in how the former colonies were governed and in their habits. After much robust argument, the confederate states concluded that they would be better off in every sense — economically, militarily and socially — if they further integrated into a federation, than if they were to continue severally in a group of thirteen more loosely associated nation-states.

Looking back a mere 225 years later, we observe how dramatically conditions have changed rendering the former concerns irrelevant. It is conceivable then, given the enormous advances in communications and transportation that modern science has placed at the disposal of our modern-day society, that federating the world will actually be an easier task than federating the United States was, and that unifying the nations of the world might prove to be less complex than what the nascent American states faced, even though the states had more in common when it came to certain traditions and language.

Another aspect of the American experience that should not be overlooked, however, is the immense suffering that accompanied the deepening of the American federation in the second half of the nineteenth century. After all, it took a violent civil war that almost tore the American Republic apart to weld the disparate colonies into a nation, rather than a mere union of independent states. We must be willing to prepare ourselves for a difficult and thorny road ahead, as it seems highly improbable that we can bring about deep and fundamental changes in the structure of society by relying solely on diplomacy and education. We must prepare ourselves for intense physical as well as mental suffering, which seem to precede and accompany historic changes that mark the greatest milestones in the history of human civilization. It is likely that we will have to suffer major global upheavals and catastrophes, unprecedented in their severity and intensity, before we can weld the currently disunified nations of our world into a cohesive world federation. The fires of global ordeals might well be needed to prepare us as a collective whole, for the next step in our social evolution, and to instill in our leaders the sense of responsibility and the mettle that they will need to lead us.

The European Coal and Steel Community and the European Union

In addition to the American experience, the world has, since the middle of the twentieth century, had the opportunity to observe and learn from the grand European experiment: Europe's slow and tortuous move towards what probably, will ultimately become a United States of Europe. Indeed, it is hard to believe that it was only as recently as 1952 that the first institution, namely the European Coal and Steel Community (ECSC), constituting the foundation of what we know today as the European Union was created. This institution provided a forum for the French and Germans to collaborate on a matter of tremendous mutual interest to them: managing the production and distribution of coal and steel that was vital to their respective economic existence. It is harder to believe that prior to the creation of the ECSC there was a long history of intense hatred between the French and the Germans. It was not uncommon to find references in their literature to a hatred that they prided themselves on fostering from childhood and to a deep-seated belief that the animosity between them would never change and would lead them always to be at loggerheads. Their history, checkered as it was, with wars that they had fought against each other, was ample proof of their long-standing enmity. Yet, with the creation of the ECSC, war gave way to peace and collaboration on a series of projects of common interest.

Like the American experience, it took tremendous suffering in the form of a destructive and bloody Second World War for the European Union to be born. Since its birth, however, the European Union has slowly evolved as envisioned by Jean Monnet, the father of the ECSC, through a process of incremental integration, that he likened to adding links to a chain of increasing unification. Consequently, although not yet a federation, the European Union also offers us lessons about processes and institutions to emulate and to avoid.

The experience of Europe after the Second World War demonstrates that nations can and will cede sovereignty in important sectors of their economy if they are convinced that it is in their own interests to do so. Our task is to craft persuasive and cogent arguments demonstrating that it is in the interests of each and every nation to cede sovereignty in certain limited areas of jurisdiction to a supranational legislature that will serve its interests better than it can serve those interests, if it acts alone.

When the Second World War ended, the countries in Europe were entrenched in large-scale economic devastation and physical destruction. Western European nations bent all their energies towards economic reconstruction, for which they needed large quantities of coal and steel. Steel was necessary for a variety of purposes including the building of railroads, buildings, bridges, ships, vehicles and machinery. Although the demand for steel was high, there was a shortage of raw materials to produce it, especially coal to fire the steel furnaces. In short, coal and steel were the two commodities that were indispensable to the reconstruction and economic revival of Europe. The role they played in the economic development and welfare of Europe were very much akin to the role that oil, gas and nuclear energy play in the economic development of nations today. Germany had always been naturally blessed with an abundance of coal, but it had also started two World Wars on the basis of its powerful coal and steel industries. The question was what to do about German coal and steel? The victorious Western European nations that had been occupied by Germany assumed that they would have access to German coal and markets while Germany's steel output would be sharply curtailed.[9]

Germany had long been rich in coal, particularly coking coal used in steel production, and France had long coveted this coal as a crucial source of economic power and felt insecure in the face of the fundamental economic strength of industrial Germany.[10] France herself was not geologically rich in coal and relied on Germany for coal supplies. No wonder then that competition over this resource had long been a source of conflict in Europe, fuelling a desire for territorial acquisition particularly between France and Germany. The French province of Alsace-Lorraine with its iron ore deposits had changed hands between the two countries in 1871, 1918, 1940 and 1945. After the First World War, the coal-rich German district of the Saar was administered by the League of Nations from 1919 to 1935 and control of its mines given to France as compensation for German damage to French coalmines. In 1923 French and Belgian troops further occupied the coal-producing Ruhr Basin of Germany as recompense for Germany's failure to pay her quota of war reparations under the Versailles agreement that ended the First World War.[11]

In the aftermath of the Second World War, France once again needed German coal to rebuild and controlled the Saar's mines from 1945 to 1957. The continued recovery of the German steel industry set the two countries on another collision course of competition which, it was feared, would lead to another devastating war. It did not help that coal and steel were also the prerequisite of military power.

England's war-time Prime Minister Winston Churchill and U.S. President Franklin Roosevelt initially concluded that the best way to forestall Germany from amassing arms and triggering yet another war was to dismember her coal and steel industries by forcing her to deindustrialize and to cap steel production. France supported this policy, hoping that partition of Germany coupled with industrial dismemberment would permanently weaken its arch-rival.[12] French policy was to make her own economy internationally competitive, while also guaranteeing security and peace, by limiting German steel capacity and simultaneously strengthening French steel industry with access to both Germany's coking coal and her markets. France also wanted to make the Ruhr Basin an International Zone out of German control while dismantling the German steel industry.[13]

Indeed, at first German steel production was restricted by the Allied Coal and Steel Control Boards and military governments and German steel plants in certain regions were placed under the authority of the U.S. and UK military governments. Germany's historical coal and steel cartels were sundered and major companies divided to reduce concentration of economic power in the industry.[14]

The U.K. and U.S. soon realized, however, that weakening and partitioning Germany was not such a good idea: A strong, unified and economically revitalized Germany created under controlled circumstances was in Europe's best interest, as Germany had an important role to play in the economic rehabilitation of Europe.[15] A new threat also appeared on the horizon from communism and the Union of Soviet Socialist Republics. Germany was considered the perfect buffer to protect the rest of Western Europe from the threat of Soviet expansion.[16] But to serve this purpose Germany needed to be strongly and firmly within the non-

Soviet camp. This goal spurred them on to accelerate the economic recovery of Germany. With its coal and steel industries intact, by 1949, Germany was making a spectacular economic recovery. Meanwhile, France desperately needed access to Germany's coal and steel on favorable terms for its own recovery. Moreover, the idea of a reunified and reconstituted West German state added to French anxiety. In short, while worrying about how they were to get their hands on enough coal and steel to rebuild their infrastructure and revitalize their economies, each European nation was also anxious to control Germany's heavy industry and to prevent the rebuilding of a German war machine that could be used against France again. German aggression had to be kept in check ensuring that another war not be triggered because of easy access to coal and steel or because of the desire to acquire territories rich in these commodities.

The countries of Europe were at an impasse and might have remained so for a while, had it not been for a brilliant plan conceived by Jean Monnet. He was the planning commissioner for France. Monnet was incredibly wise, high-minded and insightful. Being a Frenchman, he wanted the good of his country, but he was not a nationalist in the sense that he was not willing to work for the good of France at the expense of other surrounding nations, including Germany. Monnet believed that the way to ensure the success of his and other nations in Europe was to find solutions that would benefit them all and to treat nations with a spirit of equality. He fervently believed in the common management of common problems and in working for the fusion of collective interests as opposed to trying to achieve equilibrium between competing national interests. On the basis of these principles he devised a common program of post-war production and consumption of coal and steel. The plan that he masterminded as a result represented a total shift in French policy, away from confrontation and control of

Germany towards deep cooperation with France's historical nemesis.

Monnet fervently believed that Europe would benefit from federating into a United States of Europe. However, he was wise enough to recognize that the people of that continent were not ready to embrace such an idea and would reject it. Instead, he devised a clever plan that would give European countries like France and Germany the opportunity to work in close cooperation in a narrow sector of the economy, namely coal and steel, and to jointly manage these resources. He believed that success at this experiment would give the nations of Europe the confidence, trust and desire to integrate their fortunes in other arenas, adding incremental links in a chain of ever-increasing integration leading ultimately to a European federation, even if over a long period of time.

Recognizing the central importance of coal and steel to the economic and military power of European nations and to its peace, Monnet proposed pooling the coal and steel industries of France, Germany and any other European country wanting to participate in this project under the management of a jointly-agreed supranational institution — a High Authority — that would act for the collective benefit of the member countries. A customs union and common market for these products would also be created, within which the High Authority was to ensure the supply of coal on equal terms to participating nations.[17] The institution he proposed and which came into being was known as the ECSC. The ECSC would see to it that the common market was regularly supplied with coal and steel at consistent prices and terms to consumers in all member countries and would serve as a joint buyer and seller for the community. To this end it would be empowered to collect relevant information — including how much coal and steel each nation needed and how much was being consumed — define goals and consult with representatives of the various interests.[18] The ECSC would expand and modernize the production of coal and steel and improve its quality. It would ensure that all participating member states would share the strategic resources of coal and steel and that consumers, in comparable positions within the common market, would have equal access to the commodities required, thus enabling them to rebuild their countries and economies. The ECSC would also seek the lowest prices subject to certain conditions.[19] Moreover, it would steer investment, develop common exports to other countries, and equalize and improve the living conditions of workers in the coal and steel industries.[20]

By choosing coal and steel, Monnet narrowed the project to one that was likely to be accepted by Germany and France because of its narrow economic sphere. Moreover, because of the transparency built into the ECSC, which represented the interests of all member nations, it would have the tremendous added benefit of removing the fear rife in France that Germany would once again misuse her rich resources of coal and her strong steel industry to make armaments for another European war.

Ultimately six western European nations were convinced, albeit after much vigorous debate within their parliaments, that it was in their individual self-interest to pool their coal and steel resources and act collectively than to go it alone. As a result they came together to form the ECSC, which was extremely successful but more importantly became the foundation of what we know today as the European Union and was responsible for bringing a lasting peace to Europe.

The experiences of Europe after the First and Second World Wars thus demonstrate that greater union can be—and can be recognized by political leaders and national peoples as—in the interests of each individual state. Imposing punitive reparations taxes and taking control of key industrial resources hoping to secure individual nations' economic and security needs, as seen after the First World War, does not ensure peace and can even increase the risks of war. Federation with truly joint and truly equitable control of those same resources, as seen in the creation of the ECSC after the Second World War, can achieve all those aims. And individual nations and their peoples can be persuaded to understand that their individual interests actually do lie in achieving the collective good.

WHERE ARE WE NOW?

Since the early part of the twentieth century humanity has made some strides, albeit tentative ones, in the direction of what must ultimately become a world community of federated states.

The League of Nations

In the aftermath of the First World War a League of Nations was created, the world's first experiment with a truly global institution tasked to maintain peace and avoid war. Disputes were to be negotiated rather than fought over. If that failed then economic sanctions would apply, and failing that the nations would step in and collectively fight to restore peace. Although the League did some good work, such as raising awareness of social ills and starting a campaign to eradicate leprosy and small pox, it ultimately failed to achieve its lofty goals of maintaining peace, because of a number of important flaws. Among them was that membership in the League was not universal; indeed some important countries including the United States, Germany and Russia, did not join. In addition, nations that did join refused to cede sovereignty in decision-making, requiring all decisions to be made unanimously. This weakness coupled with the fact that the League only met four times per year seriously hindered its work. These weaknesses were compounded by the members' general unwillingness to establish a standing army or even to resort to economic or military sanctions to enforce such decisions as were made to deal with recalcitrant nations. Moreover, reliant on voluntary contributions, the League's operations were chronically underfunded. As soon became apparent, the League's moral authority alone was insufficient to resolve increasingly grave threats to peace. It was no wonder then that the League ultimately failed and the world found itself embroiled in a Second World War.

The United Nations

After suffering through unimaginable horrors during the Second World War, the world realized it could not manage without an international organization tasked with maintaining the peace, and so the United Nations was created with the express purpose of serving the needs of humanity on several fronts: maintaining peace and ensuring economic and social development for all.

The United Nations has made tremendous contributions to the well-being of humanity, focusing on issues of import to millions of people around the world such as the importance of education, upholding human rights, the equality of men and women, the elimination of extremes of wealth and poverty, the maintenance of peace and security, helping those in need in times of natural disasters and famines and pandemics, promoting social and economic progress, fighting diseases and improving living standards. It has also provided an invaluable forum for nations to gather and discuss issues of collective interest, and, although disagreements abound, it strives to ensure that they are resolved without resorting to arms. Thus far the UN has saved us from the scourge of a third world war. Yet it is unclear whether in the absence of major reforms it will be able to hold back the tide of problems that threaten to engulf the world. The United Nations has hitherto been unable to find viable solutions to the greatest challenges of our time, including global warming with all its attendant problems, nuclear proliferation with all the threats it poses to the peace and security of the world, recurring instances of genocide, terrorism and overtly aggressive behavior by nations towards other nations, and potential pandemics like the Ebola virus. It is becoming increasingly evident that if the United Nations does not rise to the occasion and does not reform itself enough to solve the critical collective needs and problems of today, then it will, of necessity, be overtaken by new institutions that do.

The European Union

After the Second World War another experiment in incremental federalism began, albeit on a smaller scale. As discussed earlier, in an effort to ensure that the nations of western Europe, particularly France and Germany, had access to coal and steel to rebuild their shattered countries and economies on a fair and equal basis that did not sow the seeds of a third world war, six European nations agreed to pool their coal and steel resources and place them under the authority of a supranational agency that would make decisions that served the collective interests of all the member states. This step resulted in the formation of the ECSC, which was the precursor to what has evolved over time into the European Union of today. Although the process of evolution was slow and tortuous, moving in a repeating pattern of crisis leading to victory, it has hitherto been successful in gradually integrating the interests of its member nations, now numbering twenty-eight. Most importantly it has brought a lasting peace to Europe. At each step, when faced with crisis, members of the European communities ultimately discovered that the answer to their problems was further integration. Europe has been grappling with its latest test in the form of a recurring severe financial crisis.

As ever, the question is whether she will integrate further and move closer to a European super-state or loosen the collective bonds and disintegrate back into fragmented nation states. Meanwhile, the political turmoil next door in the Ukraine, with Crimea having seceded and been annexed by Russia and eastern Ukraine hovering on the brink of secession and annexation, has given the European Union another reason to deepen its unity by taking a united stand in the face of what it views as acts of aggression by Russia.

The world's experiments with the League of Nations, United Nations and the European Union have all been invaluable. In each of them we witness encouraging signs that we are moving towards deeper global integration. However, these experiments in global governance do not go far enough, because we have not collectively accepted the foundational principles that will enable us to build the types of collective decision-making institutions described above that are needed to address once and for all the root causes of the global challenges that beset us at this stage in our collective societal growth. The ultimate proof that these experiments have not gone far enough lies in the fact that they have not brought humanity lasting peace and prosperity or solved the most challenging global problems of our time. These experiments have, however, played a vital role in teaching us what has worked and what has not and in shedding light on the best path to take, while illuminating potential pitfalls. Strengthened by this experience, we can move confidently toward building a world federation that will encompass those collective-making institutions that we so desperately need.

WORLD FEDERATION SOLVES
GLOBAL PROBLEMS

As events in our world become more turbulent and chaotic and our global problems multiply and increase in severity, we are faced with a stark choice: we must either deepen our unity or self-destruct. Unfortunately, the fact that we appear to have skipped some developmental stages in our collective growth is exacerbating our precarious condition. We have to move quickly to catch up on the growth we have missed and begin to take speedy steps towards creating a world federation of states. The truth is that the solution to all the collective problems we face, ranging from climate change and the need for clean energy, to managing the needs of a rapidly growing world population for food, water and energy, to shoring up our global financial system to prevent its collapse, to the continuing scourges of genocide, to the proliferation of weapons of mass destruction and the behavior of rogue states that sponsor terrorism and otherwise behave aggressively towards other states, lies in the creation of a world federation—a United States of the World.

The longer we refuse to take the necessary steps to build a world federation, the more intensely we will suffer both physically and mentally. Therefore we must act now before we suffer irreversible damage from the global problems that plague us. Climate change alone has the power can wreak havoc with our world: as temperatures rise, glaciers will continue to melt at unprecedented rates, raising the level of sea water and obliterating many coastal communities and islands, including entire island-nations. The displacement of peoples that will ensue, coupled with the dwindling of arable land and sources of fresh water, will eventually lead to conflict over land, food, water and all kinds of resources. The threat of nuclear holocaust is also still with us. We must act now before we are tempted to use the nuclear weapons that still abound in a moment of anger, or they are used accidentally, triggering such a holocaust. We must act now before we have a complete financial meltdown with all the economic misery and human suffering it will entail. We must act now before our insatiable demand for energy leads us to deadly conflict over resources. We must act now before many more are killed, tortured or displaced from their homes because of the severe human rights abuses, and we must act now before a pandemic wipes out a significant part of the human race.

If we were to take each of our global challenges and envisage how they might be solved by methodically applying the principles recommended in this work and within the context of a global federal infrastructure herein proposed, we might be surprised to find that effective, actionable and efficient solutions present themselves far more easily than the scope and severity of the problems might indicate. In this chapter we shall undertake this exercise in the context of three large spheres of global challenge beginning with the European financial crisis, followed by various examples of destabilizing behavior by states that include gross human rights atrocities, nuclear proliferation and territorial aggression and ending with the dual challenges of climate change and the growing demand for energy.

The Global Financial Crisis

Starting in the 1980's the world has witnessed a succession of financial crises some of which have been more contained, affecting smaller regions of the world, and others more widespread. These crises began with the default by many Latin American countries on their debt in the 1980's, followed by currency crises in segments of the European Union in 1992-93, the Asian financial crisis in 1997-98 and the Russian financial crisis in 1998. As the number of financial crises increased, so did their scope and severity. In 2008 the world was hit by what has come to be known as the Global Financial Crisis, which led to a downturn in economic activity world-wide in the 2008-2012 global recession. This crisis and the following recession in turn contributed to a European sovereign-debt crisis from which Europe has still not recovered. It is unlikely that we have seen the last of these successive crises. Rather, it is more likely that they were merely foreshocks warning of a massive financial earthquake that is likely to wreak financial and economic havoc and cause immense suffering to humanity. Indeed, despite assertions by European leaders that they were out of the woods after the crisis, beginning in August 2014 there were rumblings pointing to a growth crisis that threatened to engulf the biggest European economies, including Germany, France and Italy. As the Economist magazine concluded the "euro crisis has not gone away; it is just waiting over the horizon."[21] Not long thereafter, reports began to surface that the European economy was experiencing extremely sluggish growth and that it risked entering a triple-dip recession, prompting deep concerns among global policy makers. Strong concerns were expressed particularly about the fact that the "Big Three" i.e. Germany, France and Italy, traditionally viewed as the largest and strongest economies of Europe, were weak. Germany, generally viewed as the economic engine of Europe barely escaped recession in the third quarter of 2014, while the French economy was languishing and Italy was in its third recession in five years.[22]

When it first occurred, the European sovereign-debt crisis sent the whole world into jitters. Six years later, global leaders were again voicing their anxiety over the inability of the European economy to revive itself after the Global Financial crisis. Why, one may ask, should the world have cared? The reason is the stark reality that all nations live in an interdependent world in which their financial destiny is inextricably woven with that of others. Financial and political leaders in countries like the United States and China acknowledged this reality as they expressed anxiety about the effect of the European crisis on their economic well-being and the dangers of a world-wide recession. World leaders sounded warnings both privately and in public that Europe's problems were dragging their nations down, too. News media echoed these concerns and their roots in world-wide interconnectivity. Thus the Economist bluntly stated "…. it is not just the euro that is at risk, but the future of the European Union and the health of the world economy."[23] Nations worried that another collapse of the financial system like the one in 2008 would reverberate around the world, dooming Europe, the United States and emerging countries to a prolonged downturn, or worse. The United States was nervous enough to send its Treasury Secretary to Europe on more than one occasion to dispense advice on the sovereign-debt crisis. His main goal was to press for decisive European action for the good of the global economy.[24] The global interdependence was on display in another way as well: Europeans hoped, albeit in vain, that China would help extricate them from the mess into which they had gotten themselves.[25]

Not surprisingly, economists, politicians, think tank pundits, academics and journalists have been trying to explain why these financial crises have occurred and how they can be avoided in the future. Their suggestions and recommendations for fixing the world's financial problems correspond directly to one or more of the principles in the proposed tool-kit for building a world federation.

Stop the Denial and Learn From Our Mistakes

Our leaders need to face the fact that both consumers and governments have been borrowing excessively and piling on debt, facilitated by banks that lent governments money by buying up sovereign bonds. Extricating ourselves from this behavior and its consequences and replacing the behavior with new, financially healthier patterns will require leaders of nations and their subjects to adjust to lower growth and to bear the pain of austerity and taxes. Unpalatable as this truth may be, and painful as these short-term remedies may be, the long-term consequence of inaction will be far more painful. Moreover, leaders need to take decisive action rather than indulge in half-measures hoping to hide the full scope of the problems, and they need to do so sooner rather than later. Commentators and analysts of the financial crisis have begun to talk openly about the need for world leaders to acknowledge their problems, to speak frankly and honestly to their citizens about them, and to stop the cycle of denial.

For example, in a number of articles over a year in 2010-2011, the Economist's regular reporting on the crisis consistently echoed these themes. In December 2010 it wrote: "Breaking up the euro is not unthinkable, just very costly. Because they refuse to face up to the possibility that it might happen, Europe's leaders are failing to take the measures necessary to avert it."[26] Seven months later in another article the Economist wrote, "For more than a year the Eurozone's debt drama has lurched from one nail-biting scene to another." It added, "Each time European policymakers reacted similarly: with denial and dithering, followed at the eleventh hour with a half-baked rescue plan to buy time."[27] Commenting in November 2011 on Greece's financial woes, it bemoaned the fact that despite warnings as early as mid-2009, Europe had engaged in denial and expediency: "... a broad pattern of denial ... helped push Greece to the brink and now threatens to pull apart the euro." The Economist laid the blame squarely at the foot of "[p]oliticians, policy makers, bankers" who "all underestimated dangers that seem clear enough in hindsight."[28]

Moreover, politicians, economists and other thinkers alike are arriving at the conclusion that we must learn from our past mistakes and not repeat them. Peter Mandelson , a former British cabinet minister said in an interview in the summer of 2012 that we should all have seen the dangers of a credit-driven period of growth and that some asset bubbles should have been dealt with earlier.[29] Former French President Nicolas Sarkozy added his voice on the need for Europe to change, warning that if it did not do so, it could be "swept away" by the euro crisis.[30]

All of these observations and comments reflect a growing understanding that human institutions, policies and laws are there to serve and safeguard the best interests of humanity and that we should not make the mistake of sacrificing ourselves and our happiness merely for the sake of upholding them. Rather, if a particular course of action, law or policy has ceased to serve us, we should have no compunction about relinquishing it and replacing it with a more beneficial substitute. Such an approach to human affairs can only be brought about as a result of inculcating within human society and our leaders a culture of learning. The above observations also reflect the need for applying the principle of honesty and forthrightness in our dealings with each other at all levels, including in the relations between our elected representatives and the people whom they serve.

Act Swiftly and Decisively

When a crisis as serious as the euro crisis looms, swift and decisive action is absolutely essential to avert disaster. Complacency is dangerous. Nor is it enough to acknowledge that there is serious danger, to avert disaster.[31] Institutions and patterns of behavior that impede swift and decisive action must be changed. Some recognized this lesson during the euro crisis. A former UK cabinet minister warned that time was running out and that the Eurozone governments had to act decisively and swiftly to save the euro, but he observed that the real underlying problem was an "engineering problem" that hindered the ability of its leaders to act swiftly.[32] News media also argued for structural change and greater integration in Europe. They noted that current European institutional procedures involve too many layers of decision-making and political complexity that interfere with the ability to react and make decisions quickly, especially in the context of fast-moving financial markets. Experts, such as Gustav Horn, Director of the Macroeconomic Policy Institute in Dusseldorf, Germany, also observed the need to streamline the decision-making process, saying that "[t]he markets see that Europe cannot decide anything quickly" which leads to uncertainty and inevitable speculation in the very financial markets that were in crisis.[33] Singapore's Finance Minister warned nations not to wait until the crisis became more severe—timely and effective action was needed. He also observed that there was a fundamental lack of confidence in the credibility of policy actions to arrest the crisis.[34]

All of these observations and warnings point to the need for effective institutions of a world federation. The world needs strong and truly representative global decision-making bodies with the authority and will to take swift and effective decisions in the collective interests of humanity. As a publication of one of the most prestigious American universities observed in its analysis of the 2008 global financial crisis, there is "one certainty" namely that "there are no localized solutions for a problem that extends throughout the world."[35]

Converge and Integrate More

Fixing the financial crisis of the Eurozone will require greater integration and convergence. As one expert put it, members of the Eurozone should have changed their economies so that they converged rather than diverged.[36] Other experts have called for deepening European integration and even creating a European Finance Ministry as the only way to solve the European financial crisis and debt problem. In the words of the former president of the European Central Bank, we need a "quantum leap" in the way the euro area is governed to avert grave crises. Already in 2011 he expressed his disappointment that leaders had not gone further.[37] Nouriel Roubini an economist widely credited with having predicted the world-wide financial crisis of 2007 – 2008, also has talked about the need to stop the disintegration and balkanization of the banking system in Europe. He argued for a fiscal union in Europe and lamented that European governments have been unable to agree to act collectively or to adopt a cohesive vision or plan.[38] Echoing his plea, there have been calls from other quarters for a banking union[39] and a more integrated monetary union that will include fiscal union and financial market union. Ultimately, said Jorg Asmussen of the European Central Bank and former German Deputy Minister of finance, "[w]e need a democratically legitimized political union" which he urges we start "speedily."[40] As expressed by Antonio Borges, director of the IMF's European unit, to put the crisis behind us, he said, "we need more Europe not less."[41]

Although these comments and advice are directed at the need to radically restructure European financial institutions, in a world that is increasingly interdependent financially and economically, we would do well to apply them at a global level as well, in a way that meets the needs of the collective interests of humanity. This is only possible if we create international institutions that represent the interests of the world and that are empowered to take the necessary decisions that conduce to those interests along with the ability to enforce them.

Adopt Legally Binding Regulations

European politicians increasingly discuss the inadequacy of legally binding and enforceable rules to regulate the Eurozone. Commenting on this fact, Chancellor Angela Merkel of Germany has said that there was a need to strengthen fiscal cooperation across the Eurozone such that it would be able to enforce controls on individual European economies. She added that "[w]here we today have agreements, we need in the future to have legally binding regulations."[42] A few months earlier, former President of France, Nicolas Sarkozy made a related point about the need for increased regulation of the financial section when he said, "we consider ... that a part of the world's woes stem from the deregulation of the financial sector."[43]

When one considers how interconnected the economies of Europe and indeed the whole world have become, it stands to reason that we cannot afford to allow individual nations to breach financial agreements with impunity, as their actions have deleterious effects on all nations. It follows that nations must agree upon financial rules and regulations that are in their collective interest, making them legally binding and enforceable. The best mechanism to do this is through a world legislature responsible for crafting the internationally applicable rules and an international tribunal that can adjudicate any disputes and make binding judgments regarding violations.

Ensure Oversight, Transparency and Accountability

Economic and financial experts, politicians and thinkers are beginning to talk about some structural changes for the financial system in Europe and eventually at the international level. These include more intrusive monitoring of banks and more transparency, accountability and corporate governance, while ensuring that creativity is not stifled. As Lord Mandelson explained, the European financial structure is not intrusive enough. Regulators need to sit in the back rooms of banks and look at their books and examine the risks the banks are taking and the possible dangers that are building up. This is especially true, he explained, in light of the rapid pace of change in financial markets with increasingly complicated and risky products being created. Lord Mandelson observed that the regulators did not keep up with the pace of change and were therefore unable to sound the warnings about the level of risk that was being built into the structure.[44]

In addition to monitoring the banks more closely, it was suggested in several quarters that stronger outside supervision and surveillance of European national budgets was necessary before they endangered the whole financial system. Indeed, the then head of the European Central bank said in December 2011 that the Eurozone needed more economic governance with tighter, more enforceable limits on debt and centralized oversight of national budgets.[45] Such oversight it was argued by some was particularly important for countries that were already in "severe difficulties."[46] Others such as the first full-time president of the European Council spoke of the need to allow the Commission the right to "intervene" as national budgets are drawn up.[47] These suggestions were subsequently implemented in Europe through a process that allows the European Commission to review draft national budgets submitted to it by Eurozone countries, to ensure that these budgets are in line with the European rules on debt and deficit. Although the new process allows the Commission to engage in a dialogue with countries whose draft budgets do not meet the agreed-upon debt and deficit limits and through that dialogue to convince European nations to adjust their national budgets to comply with the rules, in the end it still lacks the ability to enforce the rules. A patent example was the review by the Commission, of 2015 draft budgets submitted by Eurozone countries including France and Italy, in which excessive deficits were planned. After requesting additional details about the draft budgets and after intensive discussions between the Commission and the representatives of France and Italy, these two countries who had been arguing for a relaxation in the deficit limits to avoid the risks of sliding back into recession, ultimately agreed to adjust their national budgets to bring them closer to the agreed-upon deficit limits while falling short of full compliance. By making these adjustments France and Italy spared themselves the embarrassment of having their budgets returned for revisions and being declared to be in "serious non-compliance" of EU rules. However, they still risk being penalized for violating EU agreements.[48]

When countries amass such vast amounts of debt that they start to default on their loans, their economies start to spiral down, and their banks start to fail, they inevitably look to other countries and to international organizations such as the IMF to bail them out. However, these bail-outs are not cheap. Applying the principle of fairness and justice, it seems unfair for a nation to get the benefit of lax fiscal behavior and expect other countries to bail it out when it is in trouble, especially if this behavioral pattern is repeated. Viewed in this light, the Fiscal Compact reached in the Eurozone in the aftermath of the Eurozone crisis as embodied in the Treaty on Stability, Coordination and Governance in the Economic and Monetary Union ("Fiscal Compact") makes sense in that it set limits on the amount of debt and deficit that Eurozone nations can have and gives the Commission the right to monitor national budgets more rigorously and recommend changes if they pose unacceptable risks to the collective interests. In return for entering this Fiscal Compact, Germany approved the European Stability Mechanism, essentially a collective bailout package or a system in which debt is mutualized.[49]

The lessons learned from the European experience can be used to craft a fiscal system at the international level, with a World Legislature setting the rules and appointing a central regulator to oversee their implementation and ensure that they are enforced. For such a far-reaching change to be adopted by the nations of the world, it is clear that they must be willing to cede a modicum of sovereignty in this area, a step they will only take once they are convinced that their national financial interests can best be assured by guaranteeing the financial interests and health of the global community of nations.

Build a Single Centralized Regulator Able to Intervene

In the aftermath of the Eurozone crisis, not only did experts in the financial area propose regulation and monitoring, they also recommended that these tasks be carried out by a central all-seeing regulator, such as the European Central Bank, that also had the authority to intervene and would act as the lender of last resort for both sovereigns and banks.[50] To this end, in September 2012, the President of the European Central Bank (ECB) announced a new ECB bond-buying program known as the Outright Monetary Transactions. Under this program the ECB would offer to buy Eurozone countries' short-term bonds in the secondary market effectively acting as a lender of last resort for Eurozone governments in addition to its role as lender of last resort for banks. However, such purchases would be subject to strict fiscal conditions including austerity measures and required structural reforms, effectively giving the ECB the authority to intervene. These purchases would also be conditioned on a strict adherence to the provisions of the Fiscal Compact and to the European Stability Mechanism both discussed above.

Once again, the experience of the European Union can be instructive in creating the necessary fiscal and monetary mechanisms in the context of a world federal structure. One of the invaluable lessons to be gleaned is that nations must first recognize the need to cede sovereignty in certain spheres for the collective good and acknowledge that it is in their own best interests to act for the good of all. They will then be willing to create a strong Executive that will ensure that the laws and rules enacted by the World Legislature in the world's collective interest are implemented, and an International Court with compulsory jurisdiction that can issue binding judgments in cases of dispute.

Accept Coercive Enforcement

The euro crisis led the pundits to recognize that the financial structure in Europe needed to include an enforcement mechanism to ensure that the fiscal rules agreed upon were actually followed and legally enforceable; otherwise there was no point in having them.[51] This was particularly true given that part of the remedy clearly depended upon undoing certain habits developed over time that had led to laxity in financial matters. The need for enforcement was echoed by a sovereign debt expert who said, "You have to have a coercive element to make it work…" He added: "To not accept that means you are living in Alice in Wonderland."[52] Germany's Chancellor reiterated this concept and expanded on it further saying it was important to get the fundamentals of the euro right, including the development of new standards affording the European Court of Justice or the European Commission the power to reject budgets that break the rules and return them for revision.[53] The bloc's economics commissioner said that efforts were afoot to consider amending the treaties to allow penalties to be assessed on countries that violate the rules of economic discipline.[54] Mr. Van Rompuy addressed the issue with a little more specificity suggesting that the European institutions needed to be able to clamp down on countries breaching budget rules, for which he suggested considering stronger sanctions that ranged from suspending their voting rights to freezing EU funds for infrastructure projects.[55] In the end, the Eurozone countries were able to successfully reach agreement in the form of the 2012 Fiscal Compact that not only articulated clear rules about what levels of debt and deficit were to be allowed, but that also allowed penalties to be imposed on countries breaching the rules of economic discipline.

The difficult process that the Eurozone countries have had to undergo as they overcome challenge after challenge and crisis after crisis provides us with very useful lessons as we set about building a world federation. Among these is that we must give our international institutions the authority and power they need to enforce the collective decisions they have taken for the collective good. We need to create a strong International Executive that has the power to ensure that the laws passed by a World Legislature are obeyed, using coercive means if necessary.

One of the fascinating results of the soul-searching done during the euro crisis was the conclusion reached by commentators that we had had enough of short-term expedient solutions and timidity.[56] Some politicians were even been bold enough to say that it was time political leaders put aside their narrow political self-interest and acted for the collective good of their country and region. The former prime minster of Luxembourg stated the problem succinctly and honestly when he stated, "We all know what to do, but we don't know how to get re-elected once we have done it."[57]

The bane of expediency was highlighted by the difficulties reforming European treaties on financial matters (which required unanimity) in the face of concerns by Britain that these would injure its financial services industry. The Prime Minister of Britain was quoted as having said, by way of explanation "What is on offer isn't in Britain's interests, so I didn't agree to it."[58] In response to this blatant focus on self-interest, the president of the European Commission at the time was quoted as saying that Britain's demand for measures to protect its financial services industry at the December 2011 summit meeting was impossible to meet, as it would have presented a risk to the integrity of the internal market of the European Union. He added that the demand had been directly responsible for the collapse of the Europe-wide agreement meant to help save the euro.[59] As a result of Britain's position, a new agreement in the form of the 2012 Fiscal Compact was sought and reached between twenty-five of the then twenty-seven members of the European Union i.e., excluding the United Kingdom and the Czech Republic.

This event puts into relief the foundational principle for building a world federation that countries must move beyond self-interest, based on a deep understanding that it is only by guaranteeing the interests of the whole that they can assure their national self-interest. It also highlights the need when we elect members of our international institutions both to ensure that they truly represent the collective interests of the world and to structure voting procedures within these institutions so as to avoid paralysis. To this end, the voting system must be based upon and reflect the principles of oneness and equality of nations, which means that no one nation should be able to effectively veto a decision that the majority of members deem is in the best interests of the whole.

Another example of expediency that contributed to the euro crisis was the failure of the Eurozone countries to apply or enforce the Maastricht Treaty's rules limiting budget deficits to no more than 3 percent of gross domestic product and restraining overall debt to below 60 percent of annual economic output. Originally there were sanctions for exceeding these limits, but when Germany and France found themselves breaking the limits, the punishments were scrapped. Failure to apply the rules, driven by expediency and narrow self-interest, contributed to the financial mess in which Europe found itself. Ironically the Fiscal Compact eventually entered into between the seventeen members of the Eurozone and eight other European Union member states intended to rectify and prevent these problems, has at its heart the same fiscal requirements that had already been adopted in the Maastricht Treaty.[60]

This example highlights the need for our international institutions to have an enforcement mechanism that can act swiftly in the face of expediency. A strong International Executive is an important safeguard for ensuring that international rules are not disregarded by a nation or group of nations simply because they find it is in their narrowly perceived and short term self-interest to do so. The European

Commission while strong, is not yet strong enough to play this role for the European Union but then again, the European Union is not a federation and the Commission is not the kind of Federal Executive with the authority and teeth to enforce collective rules made in the interests of the Union.

Let Go of Excessive Sovereignty

The silver lining of the financial crisis and the suffering it caused is that we see the first glimmerings of awareness that solving the euro crisis requires the nations of Europe to cede more sovereignty than they already have and create a "democratically legitimized political union." [61] However, Europe is in the grips of a dilemma best articulated in the following words of a journalist: "Further union implies more sacrifice of national sovereignty than leaders of many countries wanted — let alone their voters...." [62] There is no doubt that Europe stands at another fork in the long road towards ever-deepening integration. The stark choices she faces now are either a movement much further in the direction of a federal government with common fiscal policies and involving a substantial loss of sovereignty for many nations, or a fragmentation and spinning apart with severe economic and financial consequences for all. This is a reality that is already being recognized and talked about. [63]

As EU leaders came to examine the form that this closer integration should take, one of the steps they agreed upon was to give the EU executive the power to demand changes to national budgets and essentially rewrite them before they were adopted by domestic lawmakers. Until this point, governments had only been obligated to share their national budget planning with the EU, a requirement that was, in itself, a recent innovation. As the media has noted, ceding national sovereignty over control of public finances in this way was a big stride in the evolution of the European Union, which has tried and failed through successive agreements since the euro's creation in 1999 to achieve disciplined economic convergence.[64]

Whatever decisions are ultimately taken towards further integration, the Economist correctly pointed out that everyone needs to chip in and sacrifice something for the good of the whole. The real question it suggested was not whether European leaders could save the currency, but whether enough of them were prepared to pay the price: assuming some form of joint liability for debts while also binding themselves to credible fiscal rules.[65] In other words, to avert disaster a political bargain was needed under which stronger countries would provide financial support to weaker ones in exchange for tougher rules for all. Economically strong countries like Germany feared, however, that the currency union would effectively become a transfer union in which strong economies forever support the weaker members. They insisted that if debt is to be shared, decisions on budgets and spending should also be subject to collective scrutiny. They complained that while "European leaders like to talk of mutualizing national liabilities they hate to discuss sharing national sovereignty."[66]

The Economist warned that this attitude on the part of the stronger countries needed to change or the euro would break up.[67] It suggested that the answer lay in subordinating economic sovereignty to collective discipline enforced by European technocrats in Brussels. In return for such tighter monitoring by the European Commission there might be willingness to consider increased financing by the central bank to which Germany and France are the biggest contributors.[68] Some analysts were very forthright about the nature of the decisions facing Europe, saying that "[t]he economics starts with the politics" and that leaders in fiscally healthier countries in the Eurozone, such as Germany, needed to explain to their people that bailing out failing economies like Greece was in their own self-interest and that failing to do so put their own banking system and prosperity at risk. In other words they needed to understand that acting to stem Greece's debt crisis was less an act of charity than of self-interest.[69]

Fortunately, European leaders were ultimately able to take the step towards increased scrutiny and intervention as well as mutualization of debt when they agreed to the Fiscal Compact and the accompanying European Stability Mechanism. However, the story is not yet over: despite having entered into these agreements countries continue to flout the deficit limits set particularly in the Fiscal Compact when drawing up their national budgets. For example in 2015, France, Italy and Austria amongst others failed to adhere to the deficit rules in drawing up their 2015 budgets. At the end of the day, it seems highly likely that these piece-meal steps will prove insufficient to allay the fragile state of European economies forcing the leaders of the EU to address the ultimate question of whether there will be a United States of Europe. Already, in 2011 the Economist predicted that even if Europe did not become a federation, the Eurozone would inevitably be heading for more federalism.[70] The reality is that if Europe is to muster the political will necessary to federate, she must first recognize that she must put the collective interests of her people ahead of the individual interest of any nation. Fortunately for Europe, this understanding is starting to percolate through the leadership ranks in Europe, as reflected in the comments attributed to Messrs. Barroso, Von Rompuy and Juncker respectively, that the interests of the EU as a whole must supersede the sum of its parts.[71]

The euro crisis brought to the fore another component that is critical to the success of any federal government or collective decision-making institution involving several countries, namely decision-making that is essentially fair in that it gives each nation a strong voice. Just as minorities within a nation need to be given a voice and have their needs and interests attended to for the nation to function harmoniously without grievance so deep, that minorities seek to secede from the larger whole, so too, citizens of nations within a federal structure need to feel that their nation is heard and treated equally with other nations. Ideally, one wants to avoid the kinds of feeling expressed during the euro crisis that "Germany [was] the unquestioned leader of Europe" or that "France [was] definitely subordinate to Germany" and that Britain had less influence than it had had in a long time.[72]

Federal institutions ought to be structured such that the federation's component states are fairly represented, taking into consideration factors such as population size and economic strength. We want to avoid perceptions of lack of parity and unfairness reflected in the following statements made by a senior diplomat in the context of the euro crisis, saying that it would be difficult for Europe to acknowledge that "more Europe means more centralized institutions with more power, and that means more Germany" and that "[t]o agree to a more supranational Europe is also to agree to more German leadership in Europe." He added that it would be particularly difficult for France to face this reality partly because it is so much weaker economically than Germany, which has overcome many of its problems from forging a united Germany and has since emerged bigger and stronger.[73] As it turned out, Germany's growth slowed down significantly a couple of years after those statements were made. Regardless, one can see how the underlying concern of unfairness expressed in the context of a more integrated Europe could just as easily surface in the context of a world federation, unless safeguards are put in place when establishing the infrastructure, to ensure that all the component member states are fairly represented and that their needs are given fair consideration.

Ultimately, nations will only be convinced to cede enough sovereignty in certain defined spheres if they are convinced that the federal bodies to which they are ceding the power will base decisions on the collective interest of all the nations rather than on what is good for some. Without such assurance, trust requisite for success will simply not be there.

Replace Unanimity with Majority Voting

One way to address the concern that decisions be taken for the collective good is to structure voting within federal bodies on a majority basis rather than requiring unanimity, which in practice amounts to a veto for any given country. In this regard, French President Sarkozy was on the right track when saying that to promote faster change and more fiscal responsibility, France favored more majority voting within the Eurozone instead of acting only by unanimity.[74] He said this because he fundamentally understood that it was in France's self-interest to have such a structure. This understanding is reflected in his statement that "the disappearance of the euro would make our debt unmanageable…and create a loss of confidence that would lead to paralysis and the impoverishment of France."[75]

Weak Governance Structure Must Change

Underlying the lessons of the financial crisis in Europe is the deeper lesson that Europe's problem is not about money but about structure. An eminent economics professor at Harvard went to the heart of the problem when he said, "This is a deep constitutional and institutional problem in Europe" and added "It's not a funding problem." To solve the euro crisis, the Europeans "need to take a big step toward economic and political union, whoever wants to be a part of it." He further commented that Germany was "right to hold out for systemic changes." Interestingly, he also commented that Europe needed to act quickly as she did not have the luxury of lots of time to integrate more fully – a luxury she thought she had.[76] The steps taken by Europe in the aftermath of the euro crisis to enter into a Fiscal Compact and create a European Stability Mechanism, while important, are already proving insufficient to prevent European countries, including Germany the vaunted economic engine of Europe, from sliding towards recession and in some cases sinking further into it. Clearly more far-reaching changes are needed.

Fortunately, the concept of structural change to deepen integration is beginning to be discussed openly by politicians, thinkers and journalists alike. In a panel discussion on news network France 24, a Paris-based journalist talked of a need for a federated Europe.[77] In a speech given to faculty at Cambridge University, Viviane Reding, vice-president of the European Commission revived Winston Churchill's famous in a speech he gave in Zurich in 1946 for a "United States of Europe" by making a similar call for the eighteen Eurozone countries to form a full fiscal and political union.[78]

The German Chancellor has also been talking about the need to take steps towards a closer political and economic union. Solving the fiscal crisis requires sharing the debt but that can only work she contends if there is shared decision-making over budgets, taxes and pensions.[79] This is why she is pushing to move ahead with the long-stalled process of European integration. As a former German foreign minister had said "You can't mutualize debt without mutualizing sovereignty; you can't have the financial benefits of a state without having one."[80]

Ultimately, fixing the fundamental structure in Europe requires imposing taxes on a European level, a step that has been proposed by Germany, coupled with centralized over-sight of national budgets and sanctions for profligate nations. It also requires more progress towards a "political union" in which the European Commission acts more as a European government / executive and with a stronger European Parliament holding the Commission to account. Germany has suggested that only if these kinds of steps are taken will she be willing to share more of her resources to help the neediest member countries.

All of this brings us back to the blueprint for a world federal system. As discussed at the beginning of this book, the system would include a World Parliament with power to enact certain laws in the collective interests of humanity and to which nations would cede certain rights to taxation. One might well imagine that a portion of those taxes would be available to bail out countries that were in financial difficulties. In such a situation, countries would not have to go on a desperate hunt for bail-out funds. Moreover, all nations would have contributed to these funds over time and in proportion to their size and strength and no single nation would feel like it was being taxed unfairly or bearing an undue burden. Moreover, there would also be a World Executive with power to monitor nations to ensure that they were implementing internationally-agreed-upon financial regulations. It would also have the authority to enforce these regulations long before nations got to the point of defaulting on sovereign debts and financial collapse.

The U.S. Experience Offers Guidance

Although it is becoming increasingly obvious that the solution to the European financial crisis is for Europe to federate, many still resist the idea of a European federation. Even after publishing a series of articles deeply analyzing the problem and concluding, among other things, that solving it requires "an act of supreme collective will," the Economist magazine rejected a "superstate" without offering any alternative, concluding merely that "there must be ways for good governments to force bad ones to keep in line that do not require the building of a huge new federal superstate."[81] Similarly, even Former President Sarkozy is reported to have said that while "Europe must be refounded and rethought.... [t]he reform of Europe is not a march toward supranationality."[82] Nowhere has the resistance to the idea of an EU superstate been more apparent, however, than in the results of the European Parliament elections held in May 2014 in which popular nationalist parties emerged triumphant.[83]

Yet Europeans also recognize the lesson of the American experience that further integration can be critical to solving Europe's financial crisis. After all, "America began life as a fiscal basket-case."[84] When the confederated states in America adopted their current Constitution, in 1789, both the federal and state governments were far behind in paying off the loans they had taken from foreign governments to finance their war of independence. One of the first goals of the newly enhanced federal government under the 1789 Constitution was to restore faith in the national credit. To that end the central, federal government assumed the states' war debts and refinanced all the debts, drawing up a new schedule of payments and interest. In the wake of the euro-crisis, Germany's council of economic experts found that the American federal government's assumption of state debts in 1790 provided a good model and used it as the basis of proposing a debt "redemption pact." The Council gained an understanding that monetary union cannot survive without fiscal union

America has also found occasion to encourage Europe to learn from America's own experience and to consider that the solution to her financial problems may well lie in further integration. Indeed in 2011 an official from a European Central Bank visiting the United States to consult with a financial official about the financial crisis in Europe was given a copy of the 1781 Articles of Confederation, which were the precursor to the current U.S. Constitution of 1789, and told that the answer to Europe's problems lay in forging a stronger and deeper union, just as America had done in the face of similar debt problems in its early years. As noted by a newspaper reporting this event, European officials were starting to find relevance in America's failed early effort to operate as a loose confederation of thirteen states. It went on to suggest that the absence of strong central coordination of the Eurozone's debt and spending policies was an important reason Europe had been unable to resolve her financial crisis, despite efforts of over a year and a half as of the time of the report.[85]

Indeed, the American experience of moving from a loose association of states to a federation demonstrates the tremendous power to solve the current world-wide financial crisis if a similar move were made on a global scale. We often forget that one of the main drivers for moving from a loose confederacy to a tighter federation was precisely the problem of the large debts that the thirteen American states had taken on during the revolutionary war and were finding themselves unable to repay.[86] During the war each state had separately borrowed heavily from foreign powers.[87] After the war, the states found themselves unable to repay what had become enormous debts. The Confederation was unable to help, because it lacked the power to impose taxes and most states were not paying their share of assessments to the confederate government. Exacerbating the problem, the states were printing their own money at will. The flood of paper money produced wild inflation in American economies.[88] The only solution was to move towards greater unity and integration by creating a federation with a central government capable of levying federal taxes that it could use to repay the foreign debts. This experience demonstrates the need for a central global government to which all nations cede certain powers of taxation.

Skepticism about deeper European federation that is often echoed when recommendations are made for a world federation, must not deter us. Nothing short of tireless and ceaseless effort and dogged determination will lead us to success. As we pursue a goal that may sometimes seem impossible, we must bear in mind that history is replete with great causes considered unattainable, but eventually successfully accomplished. Moreover, these changes can happen swiftly and unforeseen by the experts: the fall of the Berlin Wall in 1989, the disintegration of the Soviet Union in 1991 and the collapse of the apartheid regime in South Africa in the 1990's, are three such examples that occurred towards the end of the twentieth century.

Jean Monnet, considered to be the father of the European Union, was of a similar mind. He believed that to solve the great challenges of our time we need to be proactive, thinking ahead and preparing plans. For when crises come, which they inevitably do, people and leaders will eventually flounder and become indecisive. Then viable plans, that once were unthinkable, will seem worth trying.[89] By thinking ahead to find a solution, making conscious efforts to educate people about the solution, and gradually persuading them to embrace it, we help floundering people and leaders to find the solution they need when they are finally prepared to adopt it.[90]

Destabilizing Behavior by States

In today's world, states can threaten peace and stability with a wide range of destabilizing behavior. These behaviors include gross violations of human rights within a state ranging from the widespread use of torture to quell internal dissent, to the use of chemical weapons against local populations, all the way up to ethnic cleansing and genocide to eliminate segments of a population because of racial, religious, or ideological differences. All manner of human rights atrocities lead to the weakening of the internal fabric of a nation that commits them and in turn weakens the very building blocks that form our international community of nations. They also lead to the displacement of large numbers of people who end up as refugees in neighboring countries putting inordinate economic and social pressure on those communities. Other effects include the creation of local militias whose aim is to protect their people from human rights abuses. Fighting between the militias and government forces often leads to civil war and occasionally results in failed states in which governments can no longer keep order. Unfortunately, weakened or failed states become breeding grounds for terrorist groups to flourish as there is no longer a strong central authority to keep them in check.

Destabilizing behaviors also include states producing or otherwise acquiring and amassing weapons of mass destruction including chemical, biological and nuclear weapons in contravention of international laws. Any one of these activities sows the seeds of suspicion, fear and insecurity in other nations and often leads them to conclude that the only sensible antidote to assure their security is for them to acquire or produce similar weapons, thereby triggering arms races. These escalating arms races serve no purpose but to undermine peace and security. Moreover, the use of such weapons is too heinous to contemplate. They should never be used against fellow human beings and there is no excuse for any nation to have them.

Destabilizing behaviors also encompass acts of territorial aggression by one state against another. Even though history has demonstrated time and again that forcibly taking control of another state's territory never ends well and only results in creating ill-feeling, bitterness, and resentment that subsist for generations and lead to retaliation at the first opportunity, we insist on engaging in old habits, that seen in their true light, are vestiges of outmoded and immature behavior that only lead to disorder and grief.

It is worth examining each of these three broad categories of destabilizing behavior in turn and demonstrating how creating a federation of nations will help nations to rid themselves of their scourge.

Human Rights Atrocities

Among the most egregious destabilizing behaviors are gross human rights atrocities by a government against its own citizens. The world community has over time moved from adopting the position that such abuses are matters of purely internal concern to the country in which they occur, to recognizing that these abuses are morally reprehensible and that it is the responsibility of the international community to step in and protect innocent victims of such atrocities, when it is clear that their own governments are either unwilling or unable to do so unaided. Such a shift in international norms is, itself, reflective of the growing maturity of the international community as a collective whole. Despite this growing maturity and sense of responsibility, the international community has repeatedly been unable to prevent such atrocities in recent years, because it lacks the institutional infrastructure necessary to give effect to its collective wishes.

For instance, in 2003 armed conflict broke out between the central government of Sudan and residents of the western region of Sudan called Darfur. In the decade since then, acts of brutality amounting to genocide by agents of the Sudanese government against the people of Darfur have given rise to expressions of outrage and dismay by the international community. The United Nations and the African Union have also jointly operated an armed peacekeeping mission there since 2007. Despite these measures, however, the conflict continues, with the world community unable to take stronger measures to deter or stop the violence. What got in the way was expediency, namely the focus on short-term and narrowly perceived self-interest on the part of certain nations, such as China. Sudan was and continues to be an important source of much-needed oil for China, so much so that China was willing to use her veto power on the Security Council to prevent passage of a resolution condemning the genocide and imposing sanctions on Sudan, which might have jeopardized an important energy source for it.

Another recent example of human rights atrocities committed by a government against its people is the violence that has been perpetrated by the Syrian government against its own people for over three and a half years as of the writing of this book. The violence, that has included the use of chemical weapons, has led to the rise of militia groups intent on opposing the government and to a civil war that, as of November 2014, was believed to have caused at least 200,000 deaths and resulted in the displacement of a sizeable segment—by some estimates at least 42 percent—of the Syrian population.[91] Over 3.2 million Syrians are reported to be refugees in neighboring countries and an additional 6.5 million are internally displaced.[92] The resulting chaos and disintegration of Syrian society and the weakening of the central government is viewed as a threat to peace and stability in the Middle East and beyond. It has, by all accounts, created a fertile environment for the rise and training of a new generation of terrorists, such as the group known as the Islamic State in Iraq and the Levant (ISIL), whose goal it is to create a new Islamic State in Iraq and Syria and which has demonstrated its propensity for committing acts of brutal violence against Sunnis, Shiites and foreigners alike, as a means of achieving its ends. Alas, once again, as in the case of Darfur, the Security Council has found itself impotent to impose effective sanctions on the Syrian government, this time because Russia has vetoed proposed resolutions three times.[93] Moreover, despite negotiating meetings and summits of world leaders, arranged in the hopes of brokering a peace agreement, the international community has been impotent to end the violence and the suffering of the people of Syria.[94] The head of the United Nations refugee agency has commented that there appears to be no obvious path to a coherent global response; as crises multiply, the world becomes increasingly unpredictable, and there are competing priorities. Old crises in Afghanistan and Somalia continue unresolved while new ones begin. He summed up his feelings by saying, "It's overwhelming".[95]

Ultimately, it seems that nothing short of the threat of force by a united international community, backed by action, will stop the violence initiated by the Syrian government that has since degenerated into a civil war. Thus the government of Syria eventually agreed to surrender its stockpiles of chemical weapons and subject itself to international treaties regulating future production of such weapons only after governments in Europe and the United States publicly and credibly threatened direct military intervention, notwithstanding the absence of United Nations action.[96] Yet, on the other hand, the Syrian crisis continues, unabated, with mounting casualties and humanitarian crises, because the leader of Syria knows that the international community is both unwilling to and incapable of forcing him to step down or stop his brutal treatment of his people, because it is not unified, does not speak with one voice, and lacks a standing army that can enforce its collective will, were it able to muster one.

Nuclear Proliferation

Another example of state behavior that threatens the peace of the world is the illicit production and export of weapons of mass destruction, in particular nuclear weapons, in contravention of international laws prohibiting such behavior. A familiar example is that of the international community's long battle to contain North Korea's illicit production of nuclear material and weapons. North Korea initially signed the international Nuclear Non-Proliferation Treaty (NPT), which obligates nations without nuclear capabilities not to seek nuclear weapons, in return for which they are allowed access to nuclear technology and help to develop peaceful nuclear facilities designed to provide electricity and other non-military services such as radioactive chemicals for medical uses. Under the guise of seeking nuclear technology for the peaceful purpose of providing electricity to her people, North Korea pursued a parallel secret program to make nuclear weapons. After rumors about these clandestine efforts surfaced publicly in 2002, North Korea claimed a right to have such weapons, ejected inspectors of the International Atomic Energy Agency (IAEA) who were enforcing the terms of the NPT, and soon formally withdrew from the treaty in 2003. Three years later North Korea announced that it had conducted its first test of a nuclear weapon. Since then, the international community has unsuccessfully sought to persuade North Korea to give up her pursuit of nuclear weapons. Years of intermittent negotiations have resulted in agreements repeatedly broken by North Korea. Even sanctions have proved completely unsuccessful: North Korea has given up neither her nuclear bombs nor her capability to produce the plutonium and highly-enriched uranium to make such weapons. Moreover, North Korea continues to develop ballistic missiles capable of carrying nuclear warheads. As recently as the first quarter of 2014 North Korea has been reported to have test-fired a series of rockets and short- and medium-range ballistic missiles. By November 2014, the top American commander in South Korea was reported to have said that he believed North Korea had finally completed its quest to miniaturize a nuclear weapon so that it could be carried on a ballistic missile.[97] The combination of long-range missile development and the miniaturization of nuclear warheads to sit on top of such missiles has increased the number of nations that fall within the range of North Korean nuclear missiles and has raised the level of fear and threat worldwide. Moreover, North Korea has threatened "a new form of nuclear test" and has warned that she will continue to conduct drills to improve her ability to attack medium to long-range targets with nuclear weapons.[98]

As if concerns about North Korea were not enough, the international community has also had to contend with Iran's suspected pursuit of nuclear weapons. Like North Korea, Iran has built secret nuclear plants in violation of its obligations as a member of the NPT and has been unwilling to give the IAEA's international inspectors unfettered access to all her nuclear sites or to explain fully how her program solely pursues peaceful nuclear energy as opposed to nuclear weapons, in spite of repeated and escalating international sanctions. Yet again, the international community perceives the activities as a threat to peace in the region, but has been unable to effectively resolve the dilemma despite imposing international sanctions and continuing to negotiate with Iran to reach some mutually satisfactory permanent agreement. The missing ingredient and the key to quelling the threat posed by Iran's behavior, once and for all, is unity of voice, resolve and action on the part of the international community backed by the institutional infrastructure needed to support and enforce unified and collective decisions. The community of nations must be willing to establish clear rules regarding the building of nuclear facilities and must have the authority to monitor and verify that such rules are being enforced. Free and unfettered access by international nuclear inspectors must be part of a collective institutional infrastructure that acts to assure international security. Moreover, any evidence that a country has breached international rules must trigger immediate sanctions imposed in a unified manner by all nations without exception and the international community must have a Standing Army made up of forces from all countries that can enforce its bidding by force, if necessary, for the sake of maintaining peace.

Countries like Iran and North Korea continue to behave in ways that threaten the peace and stability of their regions and the world because they know they can and because they know that the international community lacks the unity and collective resolve to issue a binding ultimatum that it can then enforce, using arms if necessary. So long as this state of affairs continues, the world will be at the mercy of countries bent on pursuing nuclear weapons.

Nuclear weapons constitute just one of three types of weapons known as "Weapons of Mass Destruction." Chemical and biological weapons make up the other two categories. The use of chemical weapons against the people of Syria in 2013, during the course of a civil conflict between opposition groups and the government of Syria, eventually led to an acknowledgment by the government of Syria that it had been manufacturing chemical weapons and possessed not only chemical weapons production facilities, but large stockpiles of lethal chemical weapons. As a result of intense international pressure, an agreement was brokered under which Syria provided a list of her stockpiles and their locations and agreed to have these stockpiles removed and destroyed under the aegis of the international agency tasked with overseeing destruction of chemical weapons. Unfortunately, the world has had to rely on the good faith of the Syrian government in providing a complete accounting of all its stockpiles and facilities which, given the circumstances, was clearly not optimal. Moreover, the Syrian government fell behind in delivering the stockpiles of chemical weapons for export and destruction. Additionally, Syria then claimed that the Organization for the Prohibition of Chemical Weapons (OPCW) should be content to have her chemical weapons production facilities sealed rather than destroyed, in contravention of the international treaty governing chemical weapons which requires their destruction.[99] Syria continued to drag her heels: As of the end of September 2014 it was reported that there were at least twelve former chemical production facilities that remained to be destroyed in Syria.[100]

Acts of Territorial Aggression

The past quarter century has seen a rise in open attempts by one state to take control or annex portions of another state's territory. When Iraq invaded Kuwait in August 1990, it came as a shock to the international community that a nation could engage in such brazenly aggressive behavior at the end of the twentieth century. Consequently, a coalition of states led by the United States fought to oust Iraq from Kuwait and restored Kuwait to its rightful internationally-determined borders. Unfortunately, that successful joint effort by many states has not deterred similar territorial aggressions in the years since.

One particularly dangerous territorial dispute that has recently flared up is a long-simmering one between China and Japan over a group of islands in the East China seas known to the Japanese as the Senkaku islands (or Diyalou to the Chinese). The dispute has been coming to a boil with each country displaying increasingly belligerent behavior to mark the territory as its own. Although these islands essentially amount to an uninhabited group of rocks in the sea, what makes them so attractive and sought after, raising the stakes and prompting escalation in tension, are the rich natural resources that lie in the territorial seas around them, resources such as oil and gas. Fears have been expressed that unless this dispute is resolved soon, it may trigger a war in Southeast Asia. Recognizing the dangers involved, the two countries have agreed on a formal document in which they recognize the different positions they take over the waters of the East China Sea, including those surrounding the disputed islands. In addition, the Prime Minister of Japan has asked for a hotline to be installed between the two countries as soon as possible, in order to prevent any clashes or minor incidents between Chinese and Japanese vessels in the disputed waters escalating into a military conflict.[101] While encouraging, there is no guarantee that these tentative first steps will lead to an amicable resolution of this dispute. In the meantime, the international community, lacking an infrastructure in the form of an International Court with compulsory jurisdiction to compel the parties to submit their dispute to it, can only stand by waiting and hoping that the dispute will not lead to war in Asia. Even if the parties were to submit their dispute to the International Court, the fact that the Court has no means of enforcing its judgments due to the absence of an international Standing Army representing the international community, means that the peace and stability of the region is effectively left to the good will of the parties.

Most recently, in 2014, the world witnessed another act of territorial aggression in the form of the annexation by Russia of Crimea, a peninsula that has been part of Ukraine for the past half century. In addition, Russia moved large numbers of its troops to the border areas of eastern Ukraine, provoking fears that it would annex eastern Ukraine as well. In mid-November 2014, it was reported by NATO's senior military commander that Russia was moving scores of tanks, artillery, equipment, air-defense systems and combat troops from Russia into Ukraine, stoking Ukraine's fears that Russia was about to undertake a full-scale invasion.[102] Other countries in Europe, particularly other former members of the Soviet Union, worry of a return to the Cold War rivalry between Western Europe and Russia and question whether reductions of NATO forces after the end of the Soviet Union mistakenly assumed that Russia would not run roughshod over its neighbors. While America has cut back her troops and equipment, remaining NATO nations have also diminished their defense spending especially in light of the financial crisis and the need to make budget cuts. The former chief of staff of the British armed forces is reported to have said "With a resurgent Russia, this is a poor moment for the U.S.-led West to be weak in resolve and muscle." He further commented on the reality that ultimately Russia will look beyond diplomacy and sanctions "to see where the real check on [its] actions might come from."[103] In light of Russia's actions, however, NATO plans to bolster its presence in eastern Europe beginning with the creation of a 4,000-strong NATO spear-head brigade that can be ready by January 2016, to deploy swiftly, in a matter of days, to defend NATO's Baltic and Central European members. Although Poland had originally hoped that this force would be stationed on its territory, final decisions have not yet been made as to where the troops will be stationed. The hope is that such a brigade will serve both as a deterrent to further Russian territorial aggression and to reassure Baltic NATO members Estonia, Latvia, and Lithuania that NATO will defend them in the event of future threats by Russia.[104] In the meantime, Lithuania, unwilling to wait for NATO to act, has created her own 2,500- member strong rapid reaction force, hoping it can fend off any Russian attack while waiting for back-up from NATO.[105]

Russia's territorial aggression in the Ukraine affects not only the region. It is of global concern for a couple of reasons including the impact it has on the economy of Ukraine, which requires the injection of large amounts of money from the West. In the eastern areas where conflict has been raging between Russian separatists and the Ukrainian forces, reports estimate that the damage done runs into billions of dollars. In addition, Russia has been cutting off gas supplies to Ukraine and imposing sanctions on it in a bid to stifle its commerce. All in all, it is estimated that by the end of 2014, the Ukrainian economy will have shrunk by 10 percent, much more than anyone had apparently expected.[106] Russia's aggression against the Ukraine also has the potential to disrupt the peace and stability of the world because it is drawing other countries, including the members of the European Union and of NATO, chief among them the United States, increasingly into its orbit.

Many other border disputes around the world might erupt at any time into destabilizing conflict. They include a disputed western sea boundary between North and South

Korea that has resulted in periodic intermittent exchanges of artillery fire between the two countries in 2010 and 2014. While this border dispute has continued to escalate, with North Korea deploying short and medium range missiles and developing an intercontinental ballistic missile, South Korea has recently conducted its own missile test and successfully launched a newly developed ballistic missile capable of reaching most of North Korea.[107] Other dangerous border disputes include long-standing ones among India, Pakistan and China over Kashmir and various other regions, between Israel and Syria over the Golan Heights, and between Israel and the Palestinian Authority over Jerusalem and the borders of a proposed Palestinian state. All of these disputes as well as others continue to be potential powder kegs that can explode into violence and war that are likely to spread beyond the regions concerned, as other countries rush in to support one side against the other.

Solution: an Effective System of Collective Security

It is evident that the international community for too long has abdicated responsibility for taking the necessary steps to preserve peace and prevent conflict in the world. Alas, it is we, the common people who have suffered as a result. The solution to all of these problems lies in creating an international system of collective security that is at once strong and flexible, within the context of a world federation. This system must be capable of minimizing the risk that any nation will breach international peace and security while also providing a means for restoring the peace quickly and efficiently in the event it is breached.

Preventing a Breach of International Peace and Security

To forestall and prevent conflict and maintain the peace, several requirements should be met.

1. Create A Binding International Agreement on Collective Security

As a first step the nations of the world need to reach an international agreement whose sole purpose is to ensure the peace and security of all people. To increase chances of success, this agreement must initially be developed by a core group of world leaders recognized for their pure motives and devotion to the cause of world peace, their integrity and uprightness, their courage in seeking the benefit of humanity as a collective whole, and their willingness to persevere doggedly in service of the collective good. Once this core group reaches agreement it must seek to have it ratified by all nations to create an International Treaty in which all countries universally participate. A core provision of this Treaty must be that if a nation violates any of its terms thereby disturbing the peace, all the other nations will arise as one to force it back into compliance. This united response must be carried out pursuant to pre-determined criteria and rules arrived at and implemented collectively.

2. Limit the Amount and Type of Arms Every Nation Can Have

To minimize the risk that any nation will be tempted to breach the peace, the amount and type of arms each nation may possess must be restricted. All nations must agree, as a matter of principle, to limit the amount of arms each of them can have to the minimum they need to maintain internal order and security within their borders. This agreement must be embodied within the International Treaty. Thereafter an International Commission should be appointed to study the circumstances of each country and determine what that amount should reasonably be for each country. The Commission should undertake an investigation to determine the amount of arms each nation actually possesses. A plan should then be made for the destruction of that quantity of arms that exceeds the amount deemed sufficient to maintain internal order. Lastly, the process of arms destruction must be supervised by an internationally-appointed body, so as to ensure transparency and avoid arousing suspicion.

For this scheme to work, the agreement to limit the possession of arms must apply to all countries without exception. No country can be allowed to rely on a security exclusion to opt out, nor can any be allowed to withdraw from the agreement. Should a country be tempted to do either, its action should be regarding as a threat to the peace triggering collective enforcement action.

The International Treaty must include a provision to eliminate all nuclear weapons. There is no good reason for any nation to possess nuclear weapons. Using them is unthinkable and it is both unfair and ultimately impossible, as humanity has discovered the hard way, to confine them to a few countries. As long as even one nation has nuclear weapons, others will want them for a host of reasons, including at best the insecurity they engender in neighbors or rivals and at worst a desire to wield more power and influence in the world. In addition to eliminating existing arsenals of nuclear weapons, all nations must agree to stop developing and producing new weapons of mass destruction, as well as fissile material such as highly enriched uranium and separated plutonium that can be used to produce such weapons. Countries must also agree to put all facilities and nuclear material needed for the creation of nuclear energy under the management and control of a supranational body that will ensure that they are used solely for legitimate, peaceful ends, such as making electricity or nucleotides to meet the energy or medical demands of the planet. Doing so will eliminate the risk that a nation will secretly divert an otherwise legitimate energy-producing nuclear program to military purposes.

3. Strengthen the International Court to Make It More Effective and Trusted

Nations will inevitably have disputes, which must be resolved. Our goal should be to ensure that they are resolved peacefully, without resort to force and without degenerating into destabilizing conflicts. For this to happen nations must be required to take their disputes to the International Court of Justice. This International Court must be granted compulsory jurisdiction over all disputes among countries, to which all nations must submit without exceptions and opt-outs. Moreover, the judgments of the International Court must bind the parties to any conflict or dispute and must be enforceable by an international military force. Without such a requirement, nations might ignore the International Court's verdicts with impunity, thereby undermining its credibility and increasing the chances of conflict.

For nations to agree to strengthen the International Court in this way, the Court must command both the respect and trust of all nations. This will only happen if it is viewed as adequately representing all nations and its judges are seen to be acting fairly and in the collective interest of the community of nations. These judges must be unbiased and beyond moral reproach. The key to creating this type of confidence lies in how judges are elected to the International Court. As an initial matter, it is important that they be elected rather than appointed. One method of election that would ensure broad representation is to have each country's parliament elect two or three national representatives in direct proportion to the size of that country's population. The election of these national representatives should be confirmed both by the executive and head of state of each country. Thereafter, the representatives should elect a certain number from amongst themselves to serve on the International Court. In this way, the Court will come to truly represent all peoples and governments.

Once elected, the judges of the International Court must act independently and free of political pressure or other external interference. Their appointments should be for a fixed term and they should be banned from seeking future governmental appointments. Provisions should also be put in place to ensure that the court is adequately funded from international taxes levied by the World Legislature, that judges are paid adequate salaries and that judges are free from pressures to decide cases in favor of any given party and also from retribution thereafter, both before and after retirement.

Restoring the Peace Quickly and Effectively in the Event of a Breach

Regardless of how strong and effective a well-crafted system of collective security is, it is unlikely to forestall all conflict. There will probably be instances — hopefully rare — in which a country will be tempted to act in ways that disrupt international or regional peace. In those instances an effective collective security system must be capable of swiftly bringing the country to heel and restoring the peace, for which the system needs a strong enforcement mechanism, particularly a standing international military force.

1. Establish An International Standing Army

In the event that a nation violates one of the provisions of the International Treaty, thereby breaching the peace, or engages in behavior that threatens peace, such as sponsoring terrorist groups, engaging in gross and widespread human rights abuses or illegally producing and acquiring nuclear weapons, an International Executive established along the lines proposed earlier must have at its immediate disposal troops and equipment ready to deploy rapidly and effectively to maintain or restore the peace. Without such enforcement capability, the International Treaty is a dead letter and the Executive loses its authority, effectiveness and credibility, as we currently witness with respect to the Security Council of the United Nations, the international agency currently tasked with maintaining international peace and security. Recent history is replete with examples of the inefficacy and weakness of the Security Council. A few of these were mentioned above including the genocide in Darfur, illegal nuclear weapons programs in North Korea and Iran, and large-scale massacres and human rights abuses in Syria.

Many people and nations oppose the creation of an international Standing Army because they fear it may run amok and become a menace in the hands of a totalitarian world government. To convince these skeptics that an international Standing Army is vital to humanity's well-being and redounds to the best interests of all nations, we must apply the following three foundational principles when building such a force.

The first principle is that force still has a role to play in international relations, so long as it is used collectively, in accordance with clear and pre-determined guidelines and by collective institutions that truly represent all the nations the world. In addition, such force is to be used solely in the service of justice, as that term is defined by advance collective agreement of all nations. One of the important peacemakers of the 20th century speaks to this point, saying that sometimes war is a "powerful basis of peace" and "ruin the very means of reconstruction."[108] He goes on to say that if war is waged for a righteous purpose then "this apparent tyranny" is" the very substance of justice" and "this warfare the cornerstone of peace."[109]

An analogy that comes to mind in conveying the necessity for the occasional collective use of force is that of chemotherapy — using otherwise deadly chemicals to kill diseased tissue — to rid the body of cancer. Although many healthy cells are destroyed along with the cancerous ones, the alternative strategy of doing nothing is not a viable one. The sacrifice of some healthy cells is necessary for the greater goal of saving the patient. If we focus on ensuring that all cells stay intact, we risk losing the patient altogether.

The second principle is that national sovereignty must be curtailed. This principle was implicitly recognized in the context of the use of force, when the UN Charter was originally crafted. The framers of the Charter recognized using force would sometimes be necessary. They therefore provided for nations to enter into agreements with the Security Council to contribute armed forces, assistance, and facilities to the Council to use in the event that international peace was threatened or broken.[110] Unfortunately, because nations have been unwilling to forego their hold on absolute sovereignty, especially in the area of military power and more particularly in relation to the composition, maintenance and location of their forces, the relevant provisions of the Charter were never implemented, thereby severely weakening the Security Council from its birth.

The third principle is that the good of the part can best be achieved by assuring the good of the whole. In other words, a nation can effectively guarantee its well-being, if it assures the good of the community of nations as a whole. This means that when there is a threat to the peace or a breach thereof, the response must be a collective one, undertaken by collective institutions like a revamped Security Council or the International Executive of a world federation backed by a standing force that represents all the nations. Moreover, the response must be in accordance with rules that have been determined collectively in advance.

Once nations embrace these principles, they will more readily accept the need for a Standing Army that is independent of the whim of any one nation or group of nations and free of the bane of expediency, as it unabashedly enforces the International Treaty and upholds international law.

2. Determine the Criteria and Conditions For The Use of a Standing Army

In addition to creating an international Standing Army, it is imperative that the criteria by which such a force can act to enforce the peace be pre-determined by all nations collectively. This is important if we are to avoid some of the mistakes that were made when crafting the current UN system. For example, under the terms of the UN Charter, the Security Council may use force to restore or maintain peace when there is a threat to the peace, a breach of the peace, or an act of aggression,[111] but these terms are not defined. This is a flaw that needs to be remedied. The definition under the terms of a new collective security agreement should identify the triggering circumstances under which a Standing Army can act and should, at a minimum, include the following: gross human rights abuses such as genocide, the illicit production, acquisition or sale of nuclear capabilities in contravention of international laws, state sponsorship of terrorism, a build-up of arms, territorial aggression, failure to implement a judgment of the International Court (especially if this is likely to give rise to conflict), and breach of any provisions of the International Treaty.[112]

3. Gradual Steps Towards The Creation of A Standing Army

In moving towards the creation of a Standing Army as envisioned above, we are likely to encounter resistance from states. It may, however, be possible to propose an incremental approach that nations might find more palatable. First create regional security organizations, each with its own standing force. In this first stage all these regional standing forces would coordinate their activities as part of a loose network encompassing the planet. It will be easier for a nation to embrace this step, as experience has demonstrated that it is easier for nations to cede sovereignty over national security to a regional organization than to a broader international one. (The African Standby Force and the European Rapid Reaction Force are good examples.) This is so for a number of reasons, including the fact that language and culture are often shared in a region, thus creating more trust and understanding. Also, a decentralized regional organization tends not to raise the same fear as a distant centralized authority making decisions from afar, without adequately understanding local circumstances and potentially adverse ramifications of mistaken decisions. Moreover, each nation has a stronger incentive to collaborate in preserving regional security, because it is more keenly and directly impacted by events that go awry in its backyard. It is therefore in its self-interest to engage in efforts to keep its region secure.

Once this loosely integrated network of regional security organizations and their attendant standing forces is established and has functioned for some time, the second step can be taken. The regional security organizations should then formalize their relationship with the International Executive and make their forces available for its use. This step has the added benefit that the International Executive, with its finger on the security pulse of the planet, can allocate primary responsibility for the security of each region to the relevant regional security organization. The operating principle would be that a threat to any one nation is to be viewed as a threat to all in the region. However, before using regional force in any given situation, the regional security organization would first need the approval of the International Executive, as is currently required with regard to the Security Council under the terms of the UN Charter,[113] except in a dire emergency in which the regional security organization could act first and seek ratification later. Finally, an additional benefit in having the International Executive coordinate security activities world-wide, is that it can specify a time frame within which the regional force must solve the regional problem. If the regional force misses the deadline, the Executive can call upon other regional forces to lend their assistance. This kind of incremental solidarity in solving problems will slowly create trust and teach regions of the world to work together for the common cause of peace.

Eventually, the world would be ready for the third and final step of consolidating and integrating the various regional forces into permanent units of a truly independent Standing Army stationed in their regional locations. Such an arrangement makes operational sense in that the forces will be physically close to conflicts that might arise in their region and can therefore act more swiftly. It also makes more fiscal sense as it eliminates the costs of transporting them over vast distances and setting up new regional quarters every time there is a new conflict. At this final stage of development, these units will operate solely at the behest of the International Executive and completely independently of the individual nations or regional groups of nations. They will, however, engage in regular joint training exercises, and have integrated communications systems, compatible equipment and a shared language so that they can work together in unity in a seamless and effective fashion if needed.[114]

The Benefits of an International Standing Army

The creation of an international Standing Army will yield many benefits. Among them is deterrence: nations are likely to consider the consequences of collective action against them before they flout international laws with impunity. Another benefit is that the authority of international laws and institutions will be upheld, not just in word but also in practice. In addition, having pre-agreed rules that determine when the Standing Army can be used means that international agencies tasked with preserving the peace of the planet, like the current Security Council or the future International Executive can act quickly, decisively and effectively without vacillating to nip problems in the bud before they grow into full-blown war. There is also the added bonus that no one nation's military would be overstretched and no one nation would have to bear an unfair and disproportionate burden either financially or in human resources. Last, but not least, such a collective system will ensure that the rules are applied equally across the board to all violators of the peace.

The world is in desperate need of an effective system of collective security that will deter nations from entering into conflicts and restore the peace when it is breached. The creation of such a system is not only possible, but inevitable. It requires that a handful of enlightened and visionary leaders motivated solely by a desire for peace, enter into an International Agreement along the lines discussed herein, to create such a system. To be effective, the collective security system embodied in the International Agreement must at the very least, limit the amount of arms each nation can have, eliminate all nuclear weapons, strengthen the International Court and create an incrementally integrated international Standing Army.

Climate Change And Soaring Energy Demand

Climate Change

In no sphere of human life is the need for collective decision-making in the form of a world federation more apparent than in the sphere of climate change, which can safely be ranked as the biggest single threat that faces humanity today. If allowed to continue unabated, global warming will wreak untold damage and destroy life as we know it.

Scientists have been studying and monitoring climate change for many years. In 1988 the United Nations established an Intergovernmental Panel on Climate Change (IPCC), which brings together hundreds of top scientists from around the world to study climate change and to issue periodic reports summarizing their conclusions. The IPCC has been warning us for a while now that the temperature of the earth's surface has been rising at an unprecedented rapid rate. In its fifth assessment report, the IPCC has made it clear that this global warming is almost certainly (about 95 percent certain) directly caused by human activity that results in the release of greenhouse gases into the biosphere.[115] These gases trap heat and cause the rise in temperatures at the earth's surface. One of the largest contributors to greenhouse gases is carbon dioxide, which is released from many man-made sources, particularly the burning of fossil fuels like coal, wood, oil, and natural gas. Not only is the phenomenon of global warming real, it poses great risk to both human and natural systems and, unless steps are taken to arrest it, the IPCC warns there could be "severe, pervasive and irreversible impacts" by the middle to end of this century.[116] Global warming poses a severe threat to life on earth in many different ways: As atmospheric temperatures near the earth's surface rise, glaciers and ice-caps melt rapidly, causing the level of the world's seas and oceans to rise. The IPCC currently predicts that global sea levels will rise between three and twelve feet by 2100 unless global warming is checked.[117] For some countries a sea-level rise of just three feet spells disaster. Kiribati's thirty-three tiny islands and atolls sit just a few feet above sea level. A rise of three feet in water levels will mean that this nation, home to 100,000 people, will be submerged. The adverse effects of the rise in sea levels are already being felt in this island nation: The intrusion of salt water is contaminating fresh water supplies and ruining arable land. The President of Kiribati predicts that his country will be uninhabitable in as little as 30 to 60 years.[118] A similar fate awaits other low-lying island states such as the Maldives and Tuvalu, as well as other groups of islands like the San Blas archipelago off the coast of Panama.[119] Fiji, while not at risk of disappearing altogether, stands to lose a lot of land to the sea as well.

Unfortunately, while rising all around the world, sea levels are not rising at even rates. Differences in water temperatures, water currents, land movements, and salinity can cause regional and local highs and lows in sea level. Consequently, in countries such as Bangladesh, the seas are predicted to rise up to four times as much as the global average, i.e., by as much as thirteen feet by 2100. Even at three feet, this rise will eventually obliterate many coastal communities including large swathes of Bangladesh, resulting in the displacement of millions of Bangladeshis alone. Indeed it is estimated that as many as 50 million Bangladeshis will flee the country by 2050 if sea levels rise as expected.[120] The inhabitants of these areas will become refugees seeking new places to live inland. As the amount of land where humans can live, cultivate food and obtain clean water dwindles, those studying the problem predict that violent conflict will inevitably ensue.[121]

Even a rich and powerful country like the United States will not be immune from the effects of rising sea levels. Indeed, it is predicted that sea levels on the Atlantic seaboard of the United States will surge more than six feet, endangering large metropolitan areas like Boston, New York, Baltimore, Philadelphia and Providence, Rhode Island.[122] Miami, one of America's most populous cities, is particularly vulnerable to rising sea levels because it is built on a foundation of porous limestone.[123] Studies predict that the waters around it could rise up to two feet by 2060.[124]

In addition to elevated sea levels, global warming is causing heat waves and heavy rains. Increasingly unpredictable weather is causing crop failure in some places, drying out parts of the world like the Mediterranean region, and raising the incidence of drought and famine. On the whole, it is going to be increasingly difficult for farmers to keep up with the rising demand for food, especially in hotter climates, leading to starvation. The IPCC has also strongly warned about risks to the food supply, noting that climate change has already curtailed the output of wheat and corn on a global scale.[125] Climate change also threatens water supplies: The amount of snowpack is declining in some areas and in others seawater is beginning to pollute river water into unpotable brackish water, while also making the land around barren and unfit for cultivation. Climate change is also destroying coral reefs and forests and threatens the mass extinction of many plant, animal, and fish species.[126] Organic matter that was hitherto frozen in Artic soil is now beginning to melt, releasing more greenhouse gases that will exacerbate global warming. And yet the worst is still to come. "Nobody on this planet is going to be untouched by the impact of climate change."[127]

Despite these realities, for many years much of the public discussion on climate change has failed to focus on the facts put forward by the scientists. Rather, the conversation has centered on responding to skeptics of whether climate change is real or caused by human actions. Influencing the discussion were groups and political organizations that had their own political agendas. Scientists who tend to be more convinced by data than by opinions were frustrated that such political organizations and groups were giving the public at large the mistaken impression that climate change was not real, that it was an event in the distant future not worth worrying about today, or that it resulted from events that were beyond man's control, such as natural variations in the sun's total output or the earth's shifting orbit. Only very recently, in the face of some of the indisputable evidence that climate change is real, has dire consequences, and is a result of man-made action have media, the public and world leaders finally begun to recognize that something needs to be done and, beyond that, that we need "a global solution."[128] In its latest report, the IPCC warns that time is running out to stabilize the climate and avoid triggering catastrophic consequences and that we must make intensive efforts over the next fifteen years to achieve this goal.[129]

Soaring Demand for Energy

The challenge of global warming is complicated by a separate but intimately related challenge of our time. As the world's population grows and economies flourish, our demand for energy surges. Experts report that to sustain the kind of global economic growth that we witness today will require energy supplies to double and electricity supplies to triple by 2050.[130] In its latest report, The International Energy Agency predicts that primary energy demand will be up by 37 percent in 2040 placing a lot of stress on the world energy system.[131] On one hand, developed nations rely heavily on energy sources and electricity to fuel their economies thereby sustaining their industries and their transportation, and providing power to consumers. To this end they need access to sufficient and affordable energy. On the other hand, developing nations are striving to catch up economically, understandably so, given there is a strong correlation between the amount of electricity consumed per capita and the UN's human development index (HDI).[132] Indeed it is acknowledged that economic growth is essential to combat global poverty. To achieve economic growth in turn requires sufficient and reliable supplies of energy.[133] The reality, however, is that developing nations are lagging behind in access to energy: roughly 1.3 billion people in developing countries have no access to electricity and around 2.8 – 3 billion still rely on wood, straw, or manure to cook and meet their energy needs. Most of these people (approximately 80 percent) live in rural areas, mainly in Sub-Saharan Africa and South Asia.[134] They endure lives that breed resentment, despair and conflict. Meanwhile, 60 percent of energy is consumed by just 20 percent of the world's population

The more important question, however, is how this need for energy is being met. The answer is that much of the demand for energy (80 percent it is estimated), is satisfied by burning fossil fuels: coal, oil and gas. The International Energy Agency reported in 2014 that even with the growth in low-carbon sources of energy, "by 2040, the world's energy supply mix divides into four almost-equal parts: oil, gas, coal and low-carbon resources." This means that despite knowing that we must radically cut back on burning fossil fuels if we are to limit the increase in temperatures to 2 degrees centigrade, (the limit set by the IPCC if we are to avoid the most damaging consequences of climate change), given the rate at which we are proceeding, we will still be relying on fossil fuels for just under 75 percent of our energy needs by the year 2040.[135]

Not that long ago it was feared that oil and gas resources would run out. This fear coupled with high oil prices led to an intensive push to invest in technological innovations and oil exploration. This in turn led to discovery and development of large quantities of new resources, including oil and gas from ocean beds, the Arctic, and shale rock fields. In short, energy experts now expect that there will be more than enough oil and gas to meet the world's energy needs "as far as anyone can see."[136] Given the looming dangers humanity faces if we do not bring global warming under control, this is not a cause for celebration: We simply cannot afford to have such a large portion of the world's energy supply coming from fossil fuels.[137] And yet, the use of fossil fuels is on the rise.

Of the fossil fuels, coal is the dirtiest but is heavily used in developing countries. In India and China, the two most populous countries of the world with rapidly-expanding developing economies, coal is a major source of fuel for over 2 billion people, and there is resistance to giving it up because renewable sources of energy are not yet developed enough to act as complete substitutes for fossil fuels. As of 2011, for example, while coal supplied 69 percent of China's energy needs and oil and gas combined 22 percent, renewable sources accounted for much less, with 6 percent coming from hydroelectric sources, 1 percent from nuclear and 1 percent from other renewables. Although the Chinese government has set a goal of raising non-fossil fuel energy consumption to 15 percent of the total energy consumption by 2020, and although it is forecast that her reliance on coal will decline to 55 percent by 2040, yet her consumption of coal in absolute terms is actually expected to increase by over 50 percent between now and 2040, reflecting the tremendous growth of her energy demands.[138] The hard reality reflected in these figures explains the comment China's deputy ambassador to the United Nations was reported to have made in a Security Council debate, that his nation's economy is growing fast and still depends heavily on coal and other fossil fuels that scientists say are contributing to climate change.[139]

When we take into account that developing countries consume one fifth of the energy consumed by the developed world, it becomes clear that the question of how these countries meet their electricity demand is of immense consequence to the fate of the world. Finding clean energy alternatives for them will have to be a big part of the solution.

Of even greater concern is that the use of coal, including lignite or "brown coal" considered a dirtier, low-quality coal, is on the rise again even in eco-conscious Europe. The irony is that even though Europe has ambitious goals to reduce its carbon emissions to 80 percent of their 1990 levels by 2020, it continues to rely heavily on coal as a key source of energy and has even increased such reliance, with sixty-nine new coal-fired power stations being planned, because coal is cheaper than other forms of energy. Even imported coal has become cheaper than gas because the United States, having increasingly reduced her own reliance on coal in favor of gas produced from "fracking" shale deposits, is now exporting her excess supplies of coal to Europe. Meanwhile, Europe's capacity to extract gas from her own shale deposits is still nascent and very primitive compared to that of the United States and she is unable to import large quantities of liquid natural gas (LNG) because of a lack of infrastructure, which will take some years to build. Her other option for obtaining natural gas: importing it from Russia through pipelines, is also unpalatable, given Russia's proven propensity to use natural gas as a weapon to force customer-nations to support its political agenda.[140]

The development of technologies to extract natural gas trapped in underground shale basins through the process of hydraulic fracturing (known as "fracking"), converting vast quantities of heretofore inaccessible natural gas into new sources of considerable quantities of natural gas has not been helpful in the battle to arrest climate change. The problem is that natural gas, although cleaner-burning than oil or coal, is still a fossil fuel that releases large quantities of climate-altering carbon dioxide when burned.[141] Unfortunately, the abundance of oil and gas means that both developed and developing nations have less incentive to find alternative clean sources of energy. Indeed, the Economist predicts that gas-fired power stations "are more likely to substitute for solar panels, wind turbines and nuclear power stations" than for coal-fired power stations.[142] So, in the drive of nations to keep their economies alive and growing, they are likely to exacerbate global warming.

In a further ironic twist, the increased reliance on natural gas in the United States as a result of the push towards "fracking" means that the United States is now exporting much of its coal and some of its natural gas to Europe and other countries raising the level of dirty carbon emissions in other parts of the world.[143] Environmentalists worry that this sets the world on a dangerous trajectory that will make it impossible to control global warming with its devastating consequences.[144]

Another new source of energy that has caused excitement in countries such as Japan, is referred to as "flammable ice". This is essentially gas extracted from offshore deposits of methane hydrate in undersea hydrate reservoirs.

While such gas has already been extracted from onshore methane hydrate reservoirs, extraction from an undersea reservoir has recently been demonstrated for the first time off the shore of Japan, a country with few other energy sources that has dramatically reduced its reliance on nuclear power. Unfortunately, the long-term effects of methane as a greenhouse gas are still poorly understood.[145] It must therefore be treated with care so as not to exacerbate an already dangerous global warming crisis.

Adding to the problem of unsustainable use of fossil fuels is the reaction of certain countries in the aftermath of the Fukushima nuclear reactor disaster in Japan. Germany has decided to reduce its dependence on nuclear energy and plans to rid itself of nuclear power by 2022. Unfortunately, with clean energy sources like wind and solar so far unable to replace the large amounts of nuclear energy, Germany is turning back to atmosphere-polluting fossil fuels. Germany is using dirty coal, brown lignite and black coal, to make up for the shortfall in electricity production, increasing her mining of lignite and opening new coal-fired power stations.[146] She is also turning towards natural gas. As Prime Minister Merkel has explained, "if we want to exit nuclear energy and enter renewable energy, for the transition time, we need fossil power stations."[147]

Japan also decided to shut down 39 of its 54 nuclear reactors, which provided 30 percent of its electricity. To make up for the lost electricity, it has fired up dozens of fossil-fuel plants with billions of dollars' worth of imported coal, oil and natural gas. Given that Japan is the world's third largest user of electricity after China and the United States, the consequence for global warming is huge.[148] In light of the decisions made by Japan, Germany and a number of countries to reduce their reliance on nuclear energy in the aftermath of Fukushima, the International Atomic Energy Agency, the central intergovernmental forum for scientific and technical co-operation in nuclear matters, revised its forecasts on the growth of nuclear power as an alternative source of energy to fossil fuels. Since the Fukushima accident, the IAEA has consistently projected "lower growth of nuclear power" and a much higher demand for natural gas until at least 2030.[149] This shift will not only have deleterious consequences because it will exacerbate global warming, but commentators also warn that the growing dependence on Russia's gas supplies will increase her hold over Western Europe.

We all suffer as a result of these actions that rely on expedient i.e. short-term solutions that focus on a nation's narrow self-interest, because they only exacerbate global warming with all its horrific consequences to humanity as a collective whole. Our national leaders should be encouraged instead to come together and collectively seek ways to ensure that each nation has fair and equal access to the energy it needs to maintain economic growth while ensuring that the solutions are ecologically sustainable and do not exacerbate our climate change problems. Such collective decision-making and action can best be done in an ongoing, methodical fashion, by building a global federal infrastructure along the lines proposed in this book.

The Current Energy System Is Unsustainable

It is clear that the current system upon which we rely worldwide to support our energy needs is unsustainable because the inordinate reliance on burning fossil fuels propels our world towards an environmentally-induced catastrophe. As the International Energy Agency aptly put it, "[O]ur current energy-political trend is expensive, harms the environment and threatens security."[150] However, it is not only in its heavy reliance on fossil fuels that our energy system is unsustainable. Our current energy production and distribution system is also severely broken in a number of different ways. Consequently, it has spawned a wide range of problems all of which have been corroding the social, moral and economic fabric of the community of nations and ultimately undermining its peace and security. We shall examine some of these problems and their effects below.

Expediency and Turning a Blind Eye to Destructive Behavior

All nations, whether their economies are already developed, like the United States and European nations, or are developing, like China and India, worry that their energy needs may not be met. This anxiety seems to manifest itself particularly strongly in the developing nations whose energy needs are soaring very rapidly. The result is a frenzied rush to lock up domestic oil and gas resources (often referred to as 'resource nationalism') and to secure deals with energy-rich countries at all costs, including an unfortunate willingness to turn a blind eye to atrocities committed by those countries. We have seen this, in the example discussed above, of China's unwillingness to join the majority of other nations in sanctioning Sudan for widely documented human rights atrocities in the Darfur region, which many regarded as genocide, after having, together with some other countries, obtained rights to drill for oil in the Sudan.[151]

Both India and China have also aggressively courted Iran as a supplier of natural gas and oil, despite the multinational crisis surrounding Iran's nuclear program and its ongoing human rights violations. Indeed, Iran is the second biggest crude oil supplier to India after Saudi Arabia. India's imports from Iran are said to amount to about $12 billion annually and account for about 13 percent of its total crude oil imports.[152] In 2011 it looked like India attempted to send a strong message to Iran about her nuclear activities by pushing back against the payment system imposed by Iran. India did so despite her fears that China would step in and buy the Iranian oil that was being shipped to India, forcing India to look for more expensive alternatives.[153] Yet the drive for energy continues to be strong: India and Iran have revived discussions between them to build a strategic oil pipeline between their two countries. Whereas the last time they discussed this matter, they were considering a pipeline that would run overland through Pakistan, this time they are considering building deep sea pipelines that would pass through Oman instead. Given the huge strides made in technology for such undersea pipelines, they estimate that such a pipeline could be completed in as little as three to four years. The only remaining obstacle in their path is for Iran to reach a nuclear agreement with the west that would result in the sanctions against her being lifted.[154] Meanwhile Beijing closed a $70 billion deal with Iran for liquefied natural gas and crude oil in the fall of 2004.[155] It signed a further $3.2 billion natural gas deal in 2009.[156] China had also been eager to obtain an energy deal with Russia that would provide her with Russian oil and gas. Her efforts met with success upon the signing of a $440 billion gas deal between the two countries in May 2014, under which Russia is to supply gas through pipelines into Eastern China for thirty years. A second deal valued at approximately $284 billion was struck in November of the same year providing for Russia to supply gas through pipelines going into Western China.[157]

Wielding Oil As a Weapon: The Culture of Impunity

Oil and gas-rich countries are in the unfortunate position of being able to use their energy resources as weapons to force nations needing them, to do their bidding, or suffer denial of access or vastly increased costs. Examples of this behavior abound. For example Iran imposed a slowdown on oil tanker traffic at important border crossings between Iran and Afghanistan in late 2010 and early 2011, despite assurances by Afghani officials that the transported fuel was intended solely for use by civilians and would not be used by NATO military forces in Afghanistan, which apparently was Iran's concern. Iran's action led to a sharp rise in the price of refined fuel in parts of Afghanistan. The price of fuel increased by more than 50 percent in some provinces, in turn driving up the costs of basic commodities such as food and heating oil. Farmers in southern Pakistan who relied on diesel pumps for irrigation were hurt by the slowdown and some gas stations on major highways were also forced to shut down.[158]

Desperation on the part of many countries to secure access to oil and gas supplies has led some energy-rich nations to exert inappropriate political pressure, stooping so low as to resort to bribery, blackmail and intimidation. Such misuses have led to a culture of impunity on the part of some oil and gas-rich nations that, in response, elicits a culture of expediency on the part of the dependent countries. Consequently, the latter occasionally find it in their perceived short-term and narrowly-defined self-interest to put up with this intimidation.

Some of the best-known examples of such misuses involve Russia in its dealings with countries on its periphery that were former members of the Soviet Union, that continue to rely heavily on imports of Russian oil and natural gas and have considered closer ties with Western European nations and their more dynamic economies. In early 2006, for example, Russia threatened to cut off supply of natural gas to Ukraine if the latter did not agree to a large price increase demanded by the Russian state monopoly Gazprom. Russia followed through on this threat. Some observers believed that Russia was using her gas wealth and power to punish Ukraine for distancing itself from Kremlin control and leaning towards the European Union and NATO.[159] The cut-off lasted three days and prompted concerns about supplies to Western and Central European countries west of Ukraine, which are supplied Russian gas by pipelines transiting the Ukraine. This abusive pattern was repeated in 2014, in the aftermath of popular unrest in Ukraine, which resulted in ousting President Yanukovich for turning toward Russia and away from closer ties with the European Union. In addition to invading and annexing Crimea and supporting a separatist uprising in eastern Ukraine, Russia once again resorted to economic pressure by raising gas prices for Ukraine.[160] Secretary of State John Kerry responded to this behavior in the following words: "No nation should use energy to stymie a people's aspirations." He added, "It should not be used as a weapon. It's in the interest of all of us to be able to have adequate energy supplies critical to our economies, critical to our security, critical to the prosperity of our people."[161]

Russia similarly threatened Belarus at the end of 2006, asking it to pay more than double the price for natural gas that it had been paying.[162] Belarusian natural gas supplies were disrupted for a short while. Soon after a deal was struck in which Belarus agreed to increases in the price of natural gas, Russia halted supplies of crude oil running by pipeline through Belarus to Europe. This shut down affected supplies destined for Germany, Poland, Slovakia and Ukraine and rekindled concerns in Europe about the reliability of energy supplies from Russia.[163]

Some astute observers have commented that Russia's energy tactics have made it "impervious to criticism that once might have modified its behavior."[164]

Other countries have been even more explicit in their threats to cut off energy supplies unless customers changed their policies. Iran's President reportedly responded to suggestions in 2005 that its nuclear program be referred to the United Nations Security Council because it constituted a threat to international peace by threatening, "If Iran's case is sent to the Security Council, we will respond by many ways, for example by holding back on oil sales."[165] Similarly, in early 2006, Venezuela's Oil Minister stated that Venezuela might steer oil exports away from the United States, which at the time obtained more than 10 percent of her oil from Venezuela.[166]

Energy Supplies Cut Off Due to Political Instability

The threat that oil supplies will be cut off due to instability and political upheaval in oil-producing regions is a constant source of worry. In 2011 oil experts worried about the 1.3 million barrels a day of oil that was removed from the world market as a result of civil war in Libya. Unrest in Yemen and Syria removed another 300,000 barrels a day. The political turmoil in Yemen raised fears that terrorists would gain free reign in that country and threaten the oil facilities in neighboring Saudi Arabia. Unrest in a country like Saudi Arabia or Algeria that is a major oil producer, would lead to a huge spike in prices. Another fear is that the breakdown of order in Yemen could lead pirates to use the country as a base from which to threaten the nearby Bab el Mandeb shipping lane, through which 3.7 million barrels of oil flow per day.[167]

When oil supplies are threatened because of political upheaval, the world relies on the OPEC cartel and other oil-producing countries like Russia to step in and make up the shortfall by producing extra oil, thereby relieving pressure on the world economy. However, there is always the risk that these oil-producing countries will choose to hold back on extra production to cause a rise in the price of oil that will benefit them, at least in the short-run. The fact that the world is hostage to the whims of a handful of resource-rich countries is another source of continual anxiety and reflects the inequitable system we currently have of distributing critical energy resources.

A Source of Conflicts

The drive for access to, and control over, oil and gas resources is a leading cause of border conflicts and other conflicts between nations, as well as domestic conflicts within a country. As the competition for supplies of oil and natural gas grows, the risk of conflicts will only increase.[168] History is replete with examples of conflicts driven by the desire to secure sources of oil and gas: It was Japan's need to secure oil supplies that drove it to its fateful attack on Pearl Harbor. The desire to control Middle East oil was a factor leading the Soviet Union to invade Afghanistan in 1979. A similar drive prompted Saddam Hussein to invade and annex Kuwait in 1990.[169] Nigeria and Cameroon fought over the potentially oil-rich Bakassi peninsula in the Gulf of Guinea for more than a decade, until a United Nations-brokered deal finally induced Nigeria to withdraw troops in 2006.[170] Within Nigeria, the sub-Saharan African country with the largest proven oil reserves, disputes over oil have also caused bloodshed for many years.[171] In the Niger Delta region of the country, resistance and militant groups who had been clashing with each other and with the federal government over oil revenue, came together in 2005 to form the Movement for the Emancipation of the Niger Delta, resulting in the indiscriminate killing and displacement of tens of thousands of villagers, and the disruption of oil production—sometimes to the extent of 800,000 barrels a day.[172]

The uprising was contained in 2009 as a result of an amnesty program in which the government paid the militants to turn in their weapons. Unfortunately, however, the root causes of the conflict which included loss of livelihood, like farming and fishing, as a result of pollution and oil spills, lack of socioeconomic development, and the absence of a greater share by the local population in the oil revenue, have not been addressed, prompting concerns that the risk of the conflict recurring once the amnesty period comes to an end in 2015 is very high.[173]

In Sudan oil was a prime cause of a prolonged civil war between the government-controlled North and the oil-rich South. The $1 million per day of oil-export revenues funded purchases of arms to fight that civil war and, since resolution of that conflict, also to fight in the Darfur region, which is known to have major yet untapped oil reserves, to commit genocide. Although the civil war between North and South was resolved by creating a new state of South Sudan in 2011, conflict has continued to flare up over how to share revenues from the oil. The challenge lies in the fact that while three quarters of oil production capacity lies in South Sudan, that territory is landlocked and lacks refineries. South Sudan therefore relies both on Sudan's refineries as well as its pipelines and port in order to gain access to export markets.[174] There is also a continuing dispute about the new border between Sudan and South Sudan as each side attempts to include more oil-producing territory within its borders. This dispute has led to fighting and aerial bombardments[175] and has aptly been described as an economic war rather than just a border war.[176]

Conflict initiated by the desire for oil is by no means confined to Africa. As discussed earlier in the discussion on territorial aggression, the drive for ownership of, and access to, oil and gas in territorial waters in the East China Sea has led to one of the most tense standoffs between China and

Japan, with the potential of triggering a war in Asia.[177] The dispute is over five tiny, uninhabited islands, essentially a group of rocks, known to the Japanese as the Senkaku and to the Chinese as Diaoyu Islands.[178] Japan and China also both claim rights to the 700 square kilometer Chunxiao/Shirakaba oil and gas field found in what is known as the Okinawa Trough beneath the East China Sea.[179] In the Pakistani province of Baluchistan, the national government has been trying to exploit oil, gas and other mineral reserves, including copper in the face of armed opposition from local Balochi tribes who want more control over the natural resources in their region, including a greater share of the revenues they generate.[180] In the Caucasus, the development of Azerbaijan's oil sector has made possible a huge spike in defense reported in 2013 to be one billion dollars more than neighboring Armenia's entire state budget, thereby making the Nagorno-Karabakh dispute with Armenia more difficult to resolve, according to the International Crisis Group.[181] Disputes over natural resources have also fuelled conflicts in Burma and Indonesia's Papua province.[182]

There are other disputes of a similar nature in the South China Sea, including one over Scarborough shoal involving China and other countries such as Vietnam and the Philippines, Brunei, Malaysia, and Taiwan. Resolution of the problem has been largely hampered by China's refusal to negotiate the dispute collectively, and refusing to have an international tribunal arbitrate her claims to over 80 percent of the South China Sea. Instead, China insists on bilateral negotiations with each claimant, which gives her much more control and power because the other claimants depend inordinately on economic relations with China.[183]

Even the Arctic is not immune from competition over resources. Until recently these resources lay protected under thick layers of ice. However, melting of sea ice because of global warming is exposing hydrocarbon-rich territories that are now easily accessible and can be drilled, leading oil companies to compete for exploration rights. In Baffin Bay, on Greenland's western coast, both Danes and Canadians have raised their flags over the uninhabited Hans Island, and Russia and the United States also vie for rights in the area.[184] Moreover it is estimated that the continental shelf off northeast Greenland alone could hold oil and gas reserves similar to those on Alaska's North Slope. It is also estimated that undersea oil and gas deposits in the Arctic constitute about 25 percent of the world's untapped resources. Northern nations, including the United States and Russia, are eager for access to those resources. U.S. diplomatic cables released by the WikiLeaks website reveal that U.S. officials worry that the quest for access to these resources will lead to armed intervention some time in the future. Ownership of the North Pole has also become the source of dispute. Russia and Denmark have made competing claims to a vast area the underlying seabed around the Lomonosov Ridge in their desire to access its wealth, including natural gas deposits.[185] These claims have since prompted Canada to add her claim to the area. All three countries are trying to prove that the ridge is an extension of their respective continental shelves.[186]

One of the problems of resource-related conflicts is that once the conflict starts, revenues from exploiting the resource funds the parties to the conflict. Yet because of the prospect of large revenues that the resources bring to the victor, the parties are reluctant to give up the fight. In addition to the civil war in Sudan, a prime example was the conflict between the UNITA rebels and the Angolan government. Although the parties found ready support from the United States and the Soviet Union during the early years of the Angolan War, the conflict continued long after the end of the Cold War, as diamonds sustained the rebels and oil funded the government.[187]

Corruption and Poverty

One of the deleterious effects of the drive to control and exploit natural resources, including energy resources like coal and gas, is the "close connection" noted by one observer "between the exploitation of natural resources and the prevalence of corrupt and oppressive regimes."[188] In this regard, studies have shown time and again that countries rich in oil tend to suffer from dictatorial or unrepresentative government.[189] Controlling large and steady flows of money provides dictators with the incentive to stay in power to benefit themselves. Often the revenues generated from the extraction and sale of resources remain secret because they are unpublished or difficult to decipher from inadequate financial statements. The same holds true for payments made for the exploitation of such resources including royalties, fees and taxes. Moreover, oil and gas companies often hide the identities of their equity holders and subsidiaries, making it easy for corrupt leaders to cover up corruption in the form of bribery and embezzlement. It is no wonder that all too often, resource-rich countries are home to some of the world's poorest people: a privileged few benefit from their country's resources while ignoring the basic desires and needs of their people who remained trapped in poverty.[190]

Angola's experience is instructive. A few years ago it was reported that although oil accounted for an estimated 90 percent of the country's revenues, two-thirds of Angolans did not even have access to safe drinking water and the country was one of the world's poorest. Moreover, of the $3-5 billion annual state budget, $1 billion was reported to go missing every year. Although economists said the government had more money than it could spend, a combination of corruption, incompetence and the after-effects of the Angolan civil war seem to have conspired to make it difficult for the government to address even basic issues such as the absence of access to clean water and sewers leading to illness and death.[191] Unfortunately, despite efforts to correct the situation, recent reports suggest little has improved. As of 2012, it was reported that only half of the population had access to safe water. In rural areas that number fell to 38 percent.[192] Although oil revenue today accounts for 80 percent of the country's revenues, yet only 40 percent of the population has access to electricity, leaving the rest to rely on wood, charcoal, manure and crop residue to meet their heating and cooking needs.[193]

Another example can be found in Chad, where oil was discovered in the 1960s. Thanks partly to World Bank financing, oil finally began to flow through the Chad-Cameroon pipeline in 2003. Hoping to prevent the phenomenon known as 'the resource curse' also known as 'the paradox of plenty' (referring to the paradox that countries that are rich in natural resources, in particular non-renewable ones like oil, gas and minerals tend to fare worse in terms of development and economic growth than countries with fewer such resources, often due to mismanagement of revenues or diversion of funds into the pockets of corrupt officials), the World Bank insisted on an independent oversight committee to funnel a large portion of the oil revenues for poverty alleviation, education, and economic development into a fund for future generations of Chadians. Soon after the oil began to flow, however, the Chadian government suddenly announced that it would put more of the money in its general budget, bypassing the oversight panel, and would increase its spending on security. A United States government interagency review conducted in the first six months of the project indicated that 60 percent of a

$25 million "signing bonus" awarded to the government by ExxonMobil and its partners, had already been spent "outside of established budget procedures" the World Bank had laid down as a condition of its willingness to loan the government of Chad the money it needed to build an underground pipeline through Cameroon to export its oil. The review also concluded that "Chadian governance was weakening, civil conflict and risk of famine were increasing and parliamentary elections appear to have been postponed."[194] Eight years after the World Bank agreed to help finance the oil pipeline, the venture ended in failure: in September 2008, Chad repaid its loan to the World Bank, having failed to use its oil revenues for the purpose of eradicating poverty and uplifting the economic plight of its people.[195]

Corruption is by no means limited to Africa. Ecuador, for example, although rich in oil, ranks as one of the most corrupt countries, coming 102nd of 177 countries in Transparency International's index of corruption for 2013.[196] In Kazakhstan, which has billions of dollars in oil revenue, recent efforts to eradicate corruption are reported barely to be scraping the surface.[197] Indeed, it is now said that corruption in Kazakhstan has moved from being a problem to being systemic.[198]

Greed and Capitalizing on the Misfortunes of Others to Make a Profit

One of the problems of our current energy system is that energy-resource rich countries seem to have no compunction about capitalizing on the misfortunes of others to make money and to gain political power, focusing only on their national self-interest, expanding their geopolitical influence and the profitability of the endeavor. One example is Russia, which has been competing with Saudi Arabia, a member of the OPEC oil-producer cartel (of which Russia is not a member), to be the world's top oil-producing nation. Indeed, Russia is the world's largest energy-exporting nation, if one considers oil and natural gas together. In contrast to Saudi Arabia, which has generally refrained from using its larger oil production capacity and far larger reserves, Russia's interest appears to lie in raking in as much as she can in oil and gas revenues, without showing any interest in investing in spare capacity.[199]

Interference with Economic Growth

Over-reliance on revenues from the extraction of oil and gas resources can, paradoxically, slow a nation's economic growth. The phenomenon, which is known as "Dutch Disease," was named for the economic collapse suffered by the Netherlands in the 1950s and early 1960s after the discovery of oil off the shores of Holland.[200] When North Sea oil started to flow in Norwegian territories, the Norwegian economy similarly began to show symptoms of this disease, but the government was able to reverse it by taking oil revenues out of the mainstream economy and putting them into a trust fund for the future. Such a reversal is, however, generally difficult as it requires great discipline, sound governance, and political and economic transparency.

Lack of Transparent Information

The petroleum industry is notorious for its lack of transparency, which has led to many problems. This flaw was highlighted by none other than the Saudi Arabian oil minister Ali Al-Naimi. Speaking in 2005, he said that one of the biggest problems the petroleum industry faced was "[t]he absence of accurate and clear information...especially in vital subjects such as supply, demand, production and stockpiles."[201] While some attempts have been made to rectify this problem, as evidenced by the fact that ministers from energy-hungry consumer countries met with some of the world's large producers in November 2005 to inaugurate a new International Energy Forum and unveil a database of information provided by the world's main oil producing and consuming countries, the new system suffers from a basic flaw: It relies upon information to be submitted on a voluntary basis and does not provide timely and adequate information needed for governments to devise and agree upon long-term energy policy. As a result, oil prices remain volatile resulting in unpredictable costs to the consumers and unpredictable revenues for the producers. Heads of states and industry leaders meeting at the G-8 summit in Italy in 2009, thought more needed to be done to make the process more transparent. They pointed to the need for creating a system to provide more accurate and timely information about the state of global supply and demand, including information about inventories, reserves and production capacity.[202] One can see how creating a global federal infrastructure along the lines proposed in this book could help: within such a structure one can envision the benefits of creating an agency of the World Parliament whose job it would be to regularly monitor and collect information about sources of energy around the world and make it available on a timely basis to the international community as a whole.

Environmental Pollution and Damage To Health and Safety

A dearth of common standards for fossil fuel extraction has led all too often to massive environmental damage and health hazards. For example, in the Niger Delta, the local community has long complained that oil spilled from deteriorating old pipelines has destroyed both farming and fishing in the area.[203] After investigating these complaints, the UN Environment Program (UNEP) found that such spills had, indeed, occurred over the previous fifty years of oil operations, that they had polluted land, air and water in the region and that it would cost $1 billion to clean up the pollution caused.[204] Yet, three years after UNEP's report, as recently as the summer of 2014, the media and NGO's were reporting that little had been done to clean up the oil pollution in the Niger Delta, despite the fact that it had been severely contaminating drinking water in a number of communities, with carcinogens that were 900 times over the guidelines set by the World Health Organization.[205] Recently some African governments, including Niger, Gabon and Chad having learned the hard lessons of the havoc wreaked on their environment by outsiders grabbing their resources, are finally challenging China's major state oil companies operating in their territories, insisting that deals their predecessors had signed be revisited to avoid problems arising from gross environmental negligence. For example, Chad's oil minister closed down Chinese operations in August 2013, after discovering that they were dumping excess crude oil in open ditches south of the capital and then making local Chadians remove it without the benefit of any form of protection. African officials are increasingly demonstrating their willingness to put up resistance, even though they know they risk angering a very important trading partner, because, as Niger's oil minister, Foumakoye Gado explained, "This is all we've got." He added "If our natural resources are given away, we'll never get out of this."[206]

In South America, environmentalists warn that Brazil faces large-scale damage to its environment, including additional deforestation, if it proceeds with plans to lay a series of pipelines to access huge reserves of oil and gas that have been discovered in the Amazon, energy that Brazil needs to keep its economy going.[207]

Developed countries are also at risk for environmental damage. In January 2013, Canadian researchers released a study claiming that the levels of cancer-causing compounds in lakes surrounding Alberta's oil sands had risen as a result of their development. The open-bit mining involved in most oil sand production allows chemicals to become airborne, and the upgraders that separate oil bitumen from its surrounding sand emit PAHs that end up in vast wastewater ponds that eventually leak PAHs and other chemicals into downstream bodies of water.[208]

Another major cause for concern in the developed world is the increased use of "fracking" as a means of extracting natural gas. Fracking involves digging horizontal wells and using high-pressure water, sand and chemicals to break up shale formations, thereby releasing the gas inside. Critics worry that chemicals used in fracking can pollute aquifers by accident, as chemicals are injected into the ground with reckless disregard to any ensuing damage that they may cause to the environment and human health.[209] Moreover, the gas released by fracking can also find its way into drinking water further contaminating the water.[210] Another concern is that fracking consumes vast quantities of water, wasting an increasingly precious resource. There is also some evidence that fracking increases the likelihood of earthquakes.[211] Given the expectation that the fraction of American natural gas that comes from shale will rise from 14 percent in 2011 to 46 percent in 2035, one can see why it is important that these concerns be addressed. Indeed, such concerns have led many regions and even some nations in Europe to delay or prevent fracking altogether.

Even offshore oil drilling is becoming more environmentally damaging, as oil companies need to explore ever farther offshore and in ever-deeper waters to find oil. For example the "sub-salt" field being developed by Brazil is ultra-deep, requiring drilling at up to three times the normal pressure for offshore oil, which increases the likelihood of accidents and major oil spills. Some of the chemicals in the extracted oil are also very corrosive and can cause damage to the environment.[212]

The disaster that occurred as a result of an explosion on the Deepwater Horizon oil rig operated by BP in the Gulf of Mexico in April 2010, brought the dangers of offshore oil drilling to the forefront of public attention. It was by far the largest accidental marine oil spill in the history of the petroleum industry. The U.S. government estimated that close to five million barrels of oil (nearly 800 million liters) was discharged into the ocean. The spill and the clean-up resulted in extensive damage to marine and wildlife habitats, to wetlands and estuaries, and to the commercial fishing and tourism industries of the northern Gulf. A White House Commission concluded that the spill resulted from "systemic" root causes and "absent significant reform in both industry practices and government policies, might well recur."[213]

Although the environmental damage wrought by the extraction of energy resources is great, by far the worst damage is caused by humanity's uninhibited burning of fossil fuels at a time when atmospheric concentrations of greenhouse gases are causing unprecedented global warming and setting off a chain of increasingly catastrophic consequences. In this context, for the world to depend on burning coal, natural gas and oil for 80 percent of its energy supply is not only unsustainable, but insane.[214]

Unstable Energy Prices and Volatility

Keeping energy prices stable is an important factor in maintaining economic and political stability within nations and in the international economy as a whole. Every major surge in crude oil prices retards global economic growth. In 2008 the finance ministers of the Group of 8 industrialized nations spent much of their two-day meeting talking about then rising prices of petroleum that were setting off street protests across the world. Their concluding communiqué pointed out that the higher prices of oil and other commodities threatened the world economy at a time when it was still weak from the collapse of the housing market in the United States.[215] Rises in crude oil prices seem to have a particularly negative effect on vulnerable economies. The Economist summed it up well in the following sentence: "Few trends cast shadows on economies and politicians like a rise in the cost of petrol."[216] In fact, as experts point out, high crude oil prices hurt not only consumers but also oil firms and producers as well.[217] Volatility is also problematic because it exacerbates the tendency of countries that need to import large quantities of oil to do whatever it takes to lock in access to oil reserves. Although the price of oil as of November 2014 in the two main contracts that set such prices worldwide has dropped, to around $83 for light sweet crude at Brent and $78 in West Texas, a problem with oil and gas is that the rise and fall of their prices are unpredictable and rely on many uncontrollable factors including security and stability of oil-producing countries and regions, rises and drops in demand, and financial speculation.

Global Federation is Key to Resolving Climate Change and Meeting Soaring Energy Demands

Arresting the unprecedented rise of global temperatures, thereby averting wide-ranging global catastrophes, while ensuring that all peoples have access to adequate amounts of energy to meet their legitimate needs are two challenges that are global in nature and therefore demand collective solutions. Humanity has tried many ways of resolving these problems and has failed. The only effective solution lies in applying the foundational principles proposed at the beginning of this work as tools in building a world federated government that truly represents the peoples of the world and that makes decisions in the collective interests of humanity.

Both climate change and meeting the soaring energy demands of a growing and economically advancing world population are global challenges that demonstrate the damaging effects of clinging to our old habits. Insisting on burning ever-increasing amounts of fossil fuels in the face of all warnings by scientists that doing so courts disaster, is like teenage resistance to sound advice during the final throes of adolescence. Unfortunately, we seem intent on prolonging our collective adolescence. Our human family must grow up and start demonstrating maturity before it does itself irreversible damage.

It is time to give up our reliance on a system of energy production and distribution based on competition, inequity, corruption and expediency, and to replace it with an equitable and efficient system that ensures all nations access to sufficient energy for the needs of their people. This we can do by pooling all our energy resources under the control of a World Legislature that will regulate the production and distribution of clean energy to satisfy the legitimate needs of all. The Legislature will be structured to represent adequately the collective interests of humanity and will take decisions that are equitable and accrue to the collective advantage of all. Both the structure of the World Legislature and the rules that govern its operations including its decision-making processes will express the principles of the oneness of nations, of even-handed treatment of all nations, and of recognizing the need of nations to cede a portion of their sovereignty so that decisions can be taken for the collective good thus ensuring the good of each nation.

Responding To Skeptics

There will undoubtedly be many skeptics who say that nations will never agree on foundational principles to build a world federation, let alone agree to a world federal government that requires ceding even a modicum of sovereignty. The historical experiences outlined in previous chapters of creating both the American federation and the European Coal and Steel Community, the foundational institution of what is, today, the European Union, give us powerful responses to help persuade them. The leap of faith the thirteen confederate states took to integrate into an American federation clearly redounded to their collective benefit, as attested by America's growing economic, military and societal strength during the more than two centuries that have since passed. Similarly, the bold and courageous act taken particularly by France and Germany, in creating the ECSC, despite a long history of deep enmity, finally brought a lasting peace to Western Europe and set it on a path of incremental integration leading to the evolution of the European Union as we know it today with all the benefits, economic and social, that it brings to its member states.

As to those who say that it is impossible to convince all nations to agree on new foundational principles of international relations, again we can respond that not only is it desirable and theoretically possible, but that such dramatic change has been successfully achieved, as recently as September 2005, and after merely a handful of years of focused effort, when all the world's leaders gathered at the World Summit in New York to mark the turn of the century, endorsed the new international principle of 'responsibility to protect.'[218]

The principle of responsibility to protect arose in 2001, when the Canadian government appointed an International Commission on Intervention and State Sovereignty to examine new ways of addressing the complex problem that arises when the people of a country suffer human rights abuses at the hands of their government either because of the inability or the unwillingness of that government to protect them. The Commission began by carefully considering the language to employ in framing the conversation. It avoided controversial language like the 'right to intervene,' which had been used in the past but had elicited strong adverse responses because of its association with colonialist aspirations and with attempts to interfere with perceived rights enshrined in state sovereignty. Instead, the Commission adopted new language to articulate a 'responsibility to protect,' under which the international community is ultimately responsible to protect those suffering from serious and irreparable harm, such as large-scale loss of life and gross human rights atrocities and who are in dire need of protection, if their own government cannot or will not protect them. The Commission offered this newly articulated principle as one around which the international community could build consensus. [219] By using new language, the Commission evoked the noble human sentiments of responsibility and protection and called for governments and leaders to rethink their previously entrenched positions as individual nations and as members of a community of nations.

Since it was first articulated in the Commission's report, the principle of the 'responsibility to protect' (now known as "R2P") has been endorsed by the United Nations High-Level Panel on Threats, Challenges and Change which acknowledged in its report that its members saw an 'emerging norm that there is a collective responsibility to protect'[220] and by the UN Secretary General in his own follow-up report.[221] The Secretary-General was very clear that although individual states have the primary responsibility to protect their own populations, if they are unwilling or unable to do so, then the responsibility shifts to the international community to act using all means, including enforcement action if necessary. Most importantly for our purposes, this newly-developed principle was endorsed by all the world leaders at their World Summit marking the beginning of the 21st century in New York City in September 2005.[222]

What is even more amazing is that it only took five years for the principle of the responsibility to protect to go from conception to gaining worldwide acceptance. Why then should we believe the international community incapable of adopting a set of universal principles such as those proposed in the earlier section of this book? The path charted by the Commission to achieve this incredible result can serve as a useful roadmap to world leaders on how to successfully achieve this goal. One feature of the roadmap involves finding creative and non-threatening ways of framing the discussion and arriving at a formulation of principles that everyone can accept without reservation or fear. Another feature is to emulate the process the Commission and its assistants adopted of traveling to every country and methodically engaging national leaders in direct conversation about the proposed principle, sharing with them their reasons for proposing and the aims and purposes they hoped to achieve, and persuading them with well-reasoned arguments that embracing R2P would serve their nations' best interests and the collective interests of humanity.

CONCLUSION – ACT QUICKLY TO AVOID DAMAGING CONSEQUENCES

That the world is being buffeted by storms of severe crises is apparent. They include a global financial crisis that has already stunted economic growth worldwide and that threatens to continue indefinitely, an environmental crisis in the form of global warming and climate change, an energy crisis, looming food and water crises, and a crisis of international insecurity encompassing a range of other challenges: nuclear proliferation, human rights atrocities and acts of terror, and increasing international and domestic conflict driven by the range of other crises.

These crises are real and require us to act swiftly to resolve them before the consequences of inaction cause inordinate suffering. However, we need to act in ways that are helpful rather than harmful.

As our turbulent, adolescent world acts out, creating ever-increasing global challenges and struggling to solve them, we see a troubling phenomenon with greater frequency in many parts of the world. Reacting to the local effects of these global challenges and dissatisfied with responses by their national political unions, many people clamor for political independence and self-determination. They separate, believing that it will afford them more control over their own destinies and will preserve them from going down with the sinking ships of the larger communities. However, their actions not only fail to solve the problems, but are positively harmful. On the one hand, the global nature of these crises demands global solutions, which cannot be found when humanity is more fragment-ed. On the other hand, causing communities to fragment into smaller and smaller units leads to disunity and strife among peoples and nations, which exacerbates problems or even creates new ones. Moreover, continuing along this path will reverse much of the progress that humanity has made in creating concentric circles of loyalty and integra-tion that are entirely compatible with each other. Continu-ing to pursue this path will only lead us backward and re-turn us at its logical conclusion to the days of tribalism. It is imperative therefore that we redouble our efforts to reverse course and put humanity back on the path of increased in-tegration rather than fragmentation.

Looking at Europe for instance, one is struck by the in-creasingly strident movement towards separatism as re-flected by the desire of the people of Flanders for further autonomy [223] even though many powers have been de-volved to their region by the central government in Brussels over the years;[224] the movement by Catalans to gain inde-pendence from Spain resulting in a symbolic referendum in which they voted on secession in November 2014, despite a declaration by the Spanish High court that such a referen-dum would be unconstitutional;[225] and the drive by seg-ments of Scotland to break away from the United Kingdom culminating in the Scottish referendum on independence that took place in September 2014. Although the Scottish people, who turned out to vote in unprecedented numbers (97 percent of the population), ultimately decided to stay within the United Kingdom, a sizeable 45 percent of the population voted to secede.[226] Perhaps more importantly, the world community waited with bated breath for the re-sults, reflecting concerns about economic disruption within Europe and a keen awareness that Scottish secession would embolden further disintegration. The Orkney and Shetland islands might have decided to secede from Scotland to remain within the United Kingdom.[227] Moreover, the Welsh and Northern Irish might also have been tempted to clamor for breaking away from the United Kingdom. Furthermore, it was feared that if the Scotts departed, the United Kingdom would lose an important pro-European contingent of its population and would be more likely to withdraw from the European Union, an outcome seen by many as unfavorable for both the European Union and the United Kingdom.

Two main factors seem to motivate the drive for separation in these events. The first is the resentment by inhabitants of regions that are relatively wealthy compared with the rest of their countrymen, who perceive themselves to work harder than their countrymen, but to be exploited to support their poorer or lazier compatriots. They resent paying more taxes and, in some case, sharing revenues from their natural resources and carrying a large share of the debt of the countries to which they belong.

The second driver is a strong desire by those most affected by the decisions of central national governments to make more of these decisions themselves rather than by distant institutions that they perceive as being out of touch with the needs of localities or minorities and applying a uniform policy without taking important regional differences into account. Central to this desire for greater autonomy is the wish to maintain cultural diversity and traditions, including the preservation and appreciation of local languages in schools.

Ultimately it appears that what really lies at the root of these justifications for separation is a genuine and legitimate desire on the part of people at the grassroots to have a reasonable say in the crafting of their own destinies. This conclusion may explain why the Scots ultimately voted to stay within the United Kingdom even though polls in the days leading up to the referendum suggested that the result might well go the other way. In an eleventh-hour bid to convince the Scotts to remain within the Union, the three main parties in the (U.K.) Westminster parliament promised Scotts greater autonomy over taxation, public spending, and more control over welfare rates.[228] This promise, which may presage a "looser, more federal United Kingdom,"[229] may well have been what saved the 307-year old Union.

The drive for a say in crafting one's own destiny is a resounding theme of our times and is abundantly evident in many parts of the world, not just Europe. It is what animates the Kurds to want autonomy within both Turkey and Iraq. It is what drove the citizens of Crimea to secede from Ukraine,[230] the people of South Sudan to secede from Sudan and create their own independent state in 2011, and the people of Eritrea to separate from Ethiopia to create a country of their own in 1993.[231] It is the same drive that has led the residents of Hong Kong to engage in large-scale and sustained protests seeking the freedom to elect their own government without interference by central authority in Beijing. It is also what drives nationalists in Tibet and Taiwan to want to secede from China.

In the context of a world in which fragmentation appears to be the current trend, the critical question to ask is will a federated world government with centralized institutions be even further out of touch with the grassroots, act unfairly or oppressively, and thereby elicit further moves towards separation and fragmentation? Or can we craft a system of federal government that allows localities and regions to have a certain amount of autonomy and freedom in tending to their legitimate local needs, while also working collectively to solve problems of a global nature that affect them all and create an increasingly unified world community?

It is critical that we answer this question, for we face a real danger that in our rush towards fragmentation as a perceived panacea for solving all difficulties, we will set off a chain reaction of increasing fragmentation into smaller and smaller parts without a well-designed link between the parts. One can see that if left unchecked, this process can easily degenerate into an avalanche of greater and greater fragmentation and balkanization generated and fed by fear resulting only in conflict and despair. In a world in which interdependence is an inescapable reality, and in which increasing global crises demand global solutions based on collective actions, the path towards fragmentation is the path to perdition rather than salvation.

The real answer to this question is for us to redouble our efforts and move quickly to reverse course by creating a federated superstate firmly grounded in the foundational principles outlined above. While allowing the world to become more deeply integrated and unified, incorporating these principles into the very fabric and processes of a world government will safeguard the legitimate needs and aspirations of the individual and of smaller communities, while also addressing the collective needs of the planet. Within such a world federation each individual will be called upon to embrace a larger loyalty that is entirely compatible with the lesser loyalty to her nation state. Moreover, such a federated state can and should be designed to meet the legitimate needs of individual populations, granting them autonomy over many issues of particular grassroots concern to them, allowing them full expression of their cultural diversity while also guaranteeing the good of the whole by requiring that the federated parts cede certain rights of decision making to the federal government in areas which concern the generality of humanity. These latter rights should appropriately include the right of individual nations to make war on each other, relying on a central army serving the whole to maintain the peace. They should include the right to manage critical natural resources, including energy resources, for the benefit of all the people of the world, thereby eliminating conflict and unequal access to sources of energy. They should also include limited tax powers to raise the funds needed to tackle global problems such as global warming. Within such a context, the particular needs of localities, regions and nations can be balanced with certain collective needs thereby satisfying all legitimate needs and expressions of diversity and removing the primary drivers of fragmentation.

A world community that achieves this level of integration will have reached the next natural step in its collective maturation and societal evolution and will be more peaceful, prosperous, secure, healthy and happy. These are goals surely worth striving for!

NOTES AND REFERENCES

1   Sherwood, Courtney. "No Fukushima Radiation in Tests Off U.S. West Coast." *Scientific American,* July 29, 2014.

2   U.N. High Commissioner for Refugees. *Syria Regional Refugee Response.* December 8, 2014. http://data. unhcr.org/syrianrefugees/regional.php (accessed December 8, 2014).

3   Nebehay, Stephanie. "Syrian Refugees Top 3 Million, half of All Syrians Displaced: UN." *Reuters,* August 29, 2014.

4   U.S. Department of State Office of the Spokesperson. "Building International Support to Counter ISIL." *www.state.gov.* September 19, 2014. http://www.state. gov/r/pa/prs/ps/2014/09/231886.htm.State; and Hammond, Philip. "Oral Statement to Parliament: Foreign Secretary on ISIL: Iraq and Syria." *www.gov.uk.* October 16, 2014. https://www.gov.uk/government/ speeches/foreign-secretary-statement-on-isil-iraq-and-syria.

5   Cooper, Helene, and Sheri Fink. "Obama Presses Leaders to Speed Ebola Response." *The New York Times,* September 16, 2014.

6   Universal House of Justice. "The Promise of World Peace." *reference.bahai.org.* Baha'i World Center. October 1985, at para 37. http://reference.bahai.org/ en/t/uhj/PWP/.

7   Evans, Gareth. "The Responsibility to Protect: When it's right to fight." *crisigroup.org.* Progressive Politics. July 31, 2003. http://www.crisisgroup.org/en/pub lication-type/commentary/evans-the-responsibility-to-protect-when-its-right-to-fight.aspx.

8   Effendi, Shoghi. *World Order of Baha'u'llah.* First pocket-size edition. Wilmette, Illinois: Baha'i Publishing Trust, 1991.

9   Dedman, Martin. *The Origins and Development of the European Union 1945-95: A History of European Integration.* London and New York: Routledge, 1996, at 58.

10 Stirk, Peter M.R., and David Weigall. *The Origins and Development of European Integration.* London and New York: Pinter, 1999, at 31.

11 Dedman, Martin. *The Origins and Development of the European Union 1945-95: A History of European Integration.* London and New York: Routledge, 1996, at 57.

12 Dedman, Martin. *The Origins and Development of the European Union 1945-95: A History of European Integration.* London and New York: Routledge, 1996, at 49.

13 Dedman, Martin. *The Origins and Development of the European Union 1945-95: A History of European Integration.* London and New York: Routledge, 1996, at 59.

14 Dedman, Martin. *The Origins and Development of the European Union 1945-95: A History of European Integration.* London and New York: Routledge, 1996, at 58.

15 Stirk, Peter M.R., and David Weigall. *The Origins and Development of European Integration.* London and New York: Pinter, 1999, at 11.

16 Dedman, Martin. *The Origins and Development of the European Union 1945-95: A History of European Integration.* London and New York: Routledge, 1996, at 49.

17 Dedman, Martin. *The Origins and Development of the European Union 1945-95: A History of European Integration.* London and New York: Routledge, 1996, at 61.

18 Goormaghtigh, John. *European Coal and Steel Community.* Edited by Anne Winslow and Agnese N. Lockwood. New York: Carnegie Endowment for International Peace, 1995, at 359.

19 *Ibid.*

20 Fontaine, Pascal. *Jean Monnet, a grand design for Europe.* Luxembourg: Office for Official Publications of the European Communities, 1988, at 19.

21 *The Economist.* "The euro zone: That sinking feeling (again)." August 30, 2014.

22 Alderman, Liz. "Eurozone Eked out Growth in Third Quarter." *The New York Times*, November 14, 2014.

23 *The Economist.* "Europe's Currency Crisis: How to Save the Euro." September 17, 2011.

24 Cooper, Helene, and Annie Lowrie. "Eyeing 2012, White House Presses Europe on Debt." *The New York Times*, December 7, 2011.

25 Bradsher, Keith. "China Signals Reluctance to Rescue E.U." *The New York Times*, December 4, 2011.

26 *The Economist.* "The Future of the euro: Don't do it." December 2, 2010.

27 *The Economist.* "Italy and the euro: On the edge." July 14, 2011.

28 Thomas Jr., Landon, and Stephen Castle. "The Denials That Trapped Greece." *The New York Times*, November 5, 2011.

29 Mandelson, Peter. *The Interview: Peter Mandelson, former British Cabinet Minister* France 24. June 14, 2012.

30 Erlanger, Steven. "French President Warns of Dire Consequences if Euro Crisis Goes Unsolved." *The New York Times*, December 1, 2011.

31 *The Economist*. "The euro zone: Is this really the end?" November 26, 2011.

32 Mandelson, Peter. *The Interview: Peter Mandelson, former British Cabinet Minister* France 24. June 14, 2012.

33 Kulish, Nicholas. "With Germany in the Fold, Slovakia is Next to Vote on Euro Fund." *The New York Times*, September 29, 2011.

34 IMF Survey Online. *IMF Members Vow to Confront Crisis, Prevent Escalation.* September 24, 2011. http://www.imf.org/external/pubs/ft/survey/so/2011/pol092411a.htm.

35 MacMillan Center. *Global Economic Crisis: Solutions.* Yale University. April 8, 2014. http://yaleglobal.yale.edu/special_report/732.

36 Mandelson, Peter. *The Interview: Peter Mandelson, former British Cabinet Minister* France 24. June 14, 2012.

37 Ewing, Jack, and Niki Kitsantonis. "Trichet Calls for E.U. Finance Ministry to Curb Future Crises." *The New York Times*, June 2, 2011.

38 Roubini, Nouriel, interview by Owen Fairclough. *The Interview: Nouriel Roubini, Economist* France 24. June 12, 2012.

39 Mandelson, Peter. *The Interview: Peter Mandelson, former British Cabinet Minister* France 24. June 14, 2012.

40 Freeland, Chrystia, and Reuters. "To Save E.U., Europe Must Believe in It." *The New York Times*, June 7, 2012.

41 Story, Louise, and Matthew Saltmarsh. "Europeans Talk of Sharp Change in Fiscal Affairs." *The New York Times*, September 5, 2011.

42   Kulish, Nicholas, and Alan Cowell. "Urging Quick Action, Merkel Says Euro Fix Could Take Years." *The New York Times*, December 2, 2011.

43   Waterfield, Bruno. "EU suffers worst split in history as David Cameron blocks treaty change." *The Telegraph*, December 9, 2011.

44   Mandelson, Peter. *The Interview: Peter Mandelson, former British Cabinet Minister* France 24. June 14, 2012.

45   Erlanger, Steven. "French President Warns of Dire Consequences if Euro Crisis Goes Unsolved." *The New York Times*, December 1, 2011.

46   *The Economist.* "Charlemagne: The Sinking Euro." November 26, 2011.

47   "Eurozone facing 'systemic crisis': Barroso." *France 24.* November 16, 2011.

48   Spiegel, Peter. "Brussels Clears France and Italy's Budgets." *The Financial Times*, October 28, 2014.

49   Sinn, Hans-Werner. *Europe's Brush with Debt.* October 22, 2014.   http://www.project-syndicate.org/commen tary/eurozone-debt-mutualization-or-individual-liability-by-hans-werner-sinn-2014-10#.

50   Mandelson, Peter. *The Interview: Peter Mandelson, former British Cabinet Minister* France 24. June 14, 2012.

51   Walker, Marcus. "Euro Zone Weighs Plan to Speed Fiscal Integration." *The Wall Street Journal*, November 26, 2011.

52   Thomas Jr., Landon, and Stephen Castle. "The Denials That Trapped Greece." *The New York Times*, November 5, 2011.

53   Erlanger, Steven. "Sarkozy and Merkel Push for Changes to Europe Treaty." *The New York Times*, December 5, 2011.

54 *Helsingin Sanomat.* "Rehn threatens rule-breaking euro countries with punishment." April 9, 2014.

55 "Eurozone facing 'systemic crisis': Barroso." *France 24.* November 16, 2011.

56 *The Economist.* "Charlemagne: Decision Time." May 12, 2011.

57 *The Economist.* "The future of Europe: Staring into the abyss." July 8, 2010.

58 Lyall, Sarah, and Julia Werdigier. "In Rejecting Treaty, Cameron is Isolated." *The New York Times*, December 9, 2011.

59 Lyall, Sarah, and Steven Erlanger. "European Commission Chief Assails Britain Over Treaty Veto." *The New York Times*, December 13, 2011.

60 BBC News. "Euro Zone Agrees to Follow the Original Rules." *The New York Times*, December 9, 2011; and Lyall, Sarah, and Julia Werdigier. "In Rejecting Treaty, Cameron is Isolated."

61 Freeland, Chrystia, and Reuters. "To Save E.U., Europe Must Believe in It." *The New York Times*, June 7, 2012.

62 Erlanger, Steven. "Necessity, Not Inclination, Nudges Europeans Closer Fiscally and Politically." *The New York Times*, June 7, 2012.

63 Norris, Floyd. "Why Not Give Greeks Their Say?" *The New York Times*, November 3, 2011.

64 "Eurozone facing 'systemic crisis': Barroso." *France 24.* November 16, 2011.

65 *The Economist.* "Europe's Currency Crisis: How to Save the Euro." September 17, 2011.

66 *The Economist.* "Charlemagne: Between two nightmares." June 16, 2012.

67 *The Economist.* "The euro zone: Is this really the end?" November 26, 2011.

68 Ewing, Jack, and Niki Kitsantonis. "Central Bank Chief Hints at Stepping Up Euro Support." *The New York Times*, December 1, 2011.

69 *The Economist.* "Europe's sovereign-debt crisis: Acropolis Now." April 29, 2010.

70 *The Economist.* "Charlemagne: Those Obstructive Brits." December 10, 2011.

71 "Eurozone facing 'systemic crisis': Barroso." *France 24.* November 16, 2011.

72 Castle, Stephen. "Crisis Batters E.U.'s Longtime Cherished Notion of Members' Equality." *The New York Times*, December 7, 2011.

73 Erlanger, Steven. "Talks May Test Partnership Between a Weak France and a Strong Germany." *The New York Times*, June 21, 2012.

74 Erlanger, Steven. "French President Warns of Dire Consequences if Euro Crisis Goes Unsolved." *The New York Times*, December 1, 2011.

75 *Ibid.*

76 Erlanger, Steven. "Money Flows, but What Euro Zone Lacks is Glue." *The New York Times*, November 30 2011.

77 Interview by Cyril Vanier. *World This Week* France 24. 2012.

78 Watt, Nicholas. "Eurozone Countries should form United States of Europe, says EC vice-president." *The Guardian*, February 17, 2014.

79 Erlanger, Steven. "Talks May Test Partnership Between a Weak France and a Strong Germany." *The New York Times*, June 21, 2012.

80 *Ibid.*

81 *The Economist.* "Europe's Currency Crisis: How to Save the Euro." September 17, 2011.

82 Erlanger, Steven. "Sarkozy and Merkel Push for Changes to Europe Treaty." *The New York Times*, December 5, 2011.

83 Pollard, Robert A. *Europe's Struggle for Democratic Legitimacy: Voters Say No to EU Super-State.* Center for Strategic and International Studies. July 10, 2014. http://csis.org/publication/europes-struggle-demo cratic-legitimacy-voters-say-no-eu-super-state.

84 *The Economist.* "Economics focus: One Nation Overdrawn: Lessons for Europe from America's History." December 17, 2011.

85 Story, Louise, and Matthew Saltmarsh. "Europeans Talk of Sharp Change in Fiscal Affairs." *The New York Times*, September 5, 2011.

86 Cerami, Charles. *Young Patriots.* Naperville, IL: Sourcebooks, Inc., 2005, at 47.

87 Cerami, Charles. *Young Patriots.* Naperville, IL: Sourcebooks, Inc., 2005, at 40.

88 Cerami, Charles. *Young Patriots.* Naperville, IL: Sourcebooks, Inc., 2005, at 38.

89 Monnet, Jean. *Memoirs.* Translated by Richard Mayne. Garden City, New York: Doubleday & Company, Inc., 1978, at pages 31, 35, 140.

90 *Ibid,* at 197.

91 Barnard, Anne. "Three Years of Strife and Cruelty Puts Syria in Free Fall." *New York Times*, March 17, 2014.

92 Global Centre for the Responsibility to Protect. *Populations at Risk: Syria.* Global Centre for the Responsibility to Protect. http://www.globalr2p.org/regions/syria (accessed 2014).

93 Sengupta, Somini. "French Push U.N. to Seek War Crimes Case in Syria." *The New York Times*, April 4, 2014.

94   Gordon, Michael R., David E. Sanger, and Eric Schmitt. "U.S. Scolds Russia as It Weighs Options on Syrian War." *The New York Times*, February 17, 2014.

95   Barnard, Anne. "Three Years of Strife and Cruelty Puts Syria in Free Fall." *New York Times*, March 17, 2014.

96   Ignatieff, Michael. "With Syria, Diplomacy Needs Force." *The New York Times*, February 25, 2014.

97   Sanger, David E. "U.S. Commander Sees Key Nuclear Step by North Korea." *The New York Times*, October 24, 2014.

98   Sang-Hun, Choe. "North and South Korea Exchange Fire Across Dispute Sea Border." *The New York Times*, March 31, 2014.

99   Sang-Hun, Choe. "South Korea Tests Missile Able to Strike Most of North." *The New York Times*, April 4, 2014.

100 Carroll, James R. "Chemical Weapons Expert Wary of Syria." *USA Today*, September 26, 2014.

101 Perlez, Jane. "For China and Japan, a New Effort to Improve Relations Produces a Chilly Scene." *The New York Times*, November 10, 2014.

102 *The Economist.* "Russia and Ukraine: Military Marches." November 15, 2014.

103 Cooper, Helene, and Steven Erlanger. "Military Cuts Render NATO Less Formidable as Deterrent to Russia." *The New York Times*, March 26, 2014.

104 McTague, Tom. "Britain to send 1,000 troops to lead new NATO 'spearhead' force based in Poland amid growing threat from Russia." *The Daily Mail*, September 6, 2014.

105 Gordon, Michael R. "Nimble New NATO Force to Take Form Next Year." *The New York Times*, December 2, 2014.

106 *The Economist.* "The Collapse of Ukraine's Economy: Don't Chicken Out of Kiev." November 15, 2014.

107 Sang-Hun, Choe. "South Korea Tests Missile Able to Strike Most of North." *The New York Times*, April 4, 2014.

108 Abdu'l-Baha. *Secret of Divine Civilization.* Pocket-size edition. Wilmette, Illinois: Baha'i Publishing Trust, 1990, at 70.

109 Abdu'l-Baha. *Secret of Divine Civilization.* Pocket-size edition. Wilmette, Illinois: Baha'i Publishing Trust, 1990, at 71.

110 United Nations. "Charter of the United Nations." *United Nations.* June 26, 1945, Articles 43 and 46. http://www.un.org/en/documents/charter/index.sht ml.

111 United Nations. "Charter of the United Nations." *United Nations.* June 26, 1945, Article 42. http://www.un.org/en/documents/charter/index.shtml.

112 Ma'ani Ewing, Sovaida. *Collective Security Within Reach.* London: George Ronald Publications, 2008, at 121.

113 United Nations. "Charter of the United Nations." *United Nations.* June 26, 1945, Chapter VIII. http://www.un.org/en/documents/charter/index.shtml.

114 For a more detailed analysis, see *Collective Security Within Reach* 159 – 168.

115 *The Economist.* "Climate Change: Of Warming and Warnings." November 3, 2014; and Intergovernmental Panel on Climate Change. "Climate Change 2014: Synthesis Report." *ipcc.ch.* Intergovernmental Panel on Climate Change. November 14, 2014. http://www.ipcc.ch/report/ar5/syr/ (accessed November 14, 2014).

116 Intergovernmental Panel on Climate Change. "Climate Change 2014: Synthesis Report." *ipcc.ch.* Intergovernmental Panel on Climate Change.

November 14, 2014. http://www.ipcc.ch/report/ar5/syr/ (accessed November 14, 2014).

[117] Intergovernmental Panel on Climate Change. "Climate Change 2014: Impacts, Adaptation, and Vulnerability." *ipcc.ch*. Intergovernmental Panel on Climate Change. March 2014. http://www.ipcc.ch/ report/ar5/wg2/.

[118] Davenport, Coral. "Rising Seas." *The New York Times*, April 5, 2014.

[119] Harris, Gardiner. "Borrowed Time on Disappearing Land." *The New York Times*, March 28, 2014.

[120] *Ibid.*

[121] Gillis, Justin. "Panel's Warning on Climate Risk: Worst is Yet to Come." *The New York Times*, March 31, 2014.

[122] U. S. Geological Survey. *Sea Level Rise Accelerating in U.S. Atlantic Coast.* June 24, 2012. http://www.usgs.gov/newsroom/article.asp?ID=3256&from=rss_home#.VhuibItFAdc.

[123] Melillo, Jerry M., Terese (T.C.) Richmond, and Gary W. Yohe. *Climate Change Impacts in the United States: The Third National Climate Assessment.* U.S. Global Change Research Program, U.S. Government Printing Office, 2014, at 841.

[124] Southeast Florida Regional Climate Change Compact Technical Ad hoc Work Group. *A Unified Sea Level Rise Projection for Southeast Florida.* Southeast Florida Regional Climate Change Compact Steering Committee, 2011, at 27.

[125] Gillis, Justin. "Panel's Warning on Climate Risk: Worst is Yet to Come." *The New York Times*, March 31, 2014.

[126] Gillis, Justin. "Climate Efforts Falling Short, U.N. Panel Says." *The New York Times*, April 13, 2014.

[127] Gillis, Justin. "Panel's Warning on Climate Risk: Worst is Yet to Come." *The New York Times*, March 31, 2014.

128 Harris, Gardiner. "Borrowed Time on Disappearing Land." *The New York Times*, March 28, 2014.

129 Gillis, Justin. "Climate Efforts Falling Short, U.N. Panel Says." *The New York Times*, April 13, 2014.

130 International Atomic Energy Agency. "IAEA Annual Report 2013." *iaea.org*. International Atomic Energy Agency. 2014.

131 International Energy Agency. *World Energy Outlook 2014*. Paris: IEA Publications, 2014.

132 Deutch, John, and Ernest J. Moniz. *The Future of Nuclear Power: An Interdisciplinary MIT Study*. Massachusetts Institute of Technology, 2003, at 19.

133 International Atomic Energy Agency. "IAEA Annual Report 2013." *iaea.org*. International Atomic Energy Agency. 2014. http://www.iaea.org/sites/default/files/anrep2013_full_0.pdf.

134 International Energy Agency. *World Energy Outlook Special Report 2013: Redrawing the Energy Climate Map*. Paris: IEA Publications, 2013; and Banerjee, Sudeshna Ghosh, et al. *Global tracking framework: Sustainable energy for all*. Working Paper, The World Bank, Washington, DC: The World Bank Group, 2013, at 289.

135 International Energy Agency. *World Energy Outlook 2014*. Paris: IEA Publications, 2014.

136 Krauss, Clifford. "There will be fuel." *The New York Times*, November 16, 2010.

137 Evans, Gareth. "Nuclear Energy in the Next Quarter Century: The IAEA's Role." *crisisgroup.org*. September 20, 2007. http://www.crisisgroup.org/en/publica tion-type/speeches/2007/evans-nuclear-energy-in-the-next-quarter-century-the-iaeas-role.aspx.

[138] U.S. Energy Information Administration (EIA). "China." *eia.gov.* February 3, 2014. http://www. eia.gov/countries/cab.cfm?fips=CH.

[139] Reuters. "U.N. Council Hits Impasse Over Debate on Warming." *The New York Times,* April 18, 2007.

[140] *The Economist.* "Europe's Dirty Secret: The Unwelcome Renaissance." January 5, 2013.

[141] *The Economist.* "Shale gas – Frack On." November 26, 2011.

[142] *Ibid.*

[143] Birnbaum, Michael. "Europe consuming more coal." *Washington Post,* February 7, 2013; and Johnson, Keith, and Ben Lefebvre. "U.S. Approves Expanded Gas Exports." *The Wall Street Journal,* May 18, 2013.

[144] Polgreen, Lydia. "Europe Turns Back to Coal Raising Climate Fears." *The New York Times,* April 23, 2008.

[145] Tabuchi, Hiroko. "An Energy Coup for Japan." *The New York Times,* March 12, 2013.

[146] Mathiesen, Karl. "New Coal power stations threat to EU's emission targets." *The Guardian,* August 27, 2014.

[147] Cala, Andres. "Russia Stands to Profit from Turn Away From Nuclear Power." *New York Times,* June 14, 2011.

[148] Tabuchi, Hiroko. "Japan Quake is Causing Costly Shift to Fossil Fuels." *The New York Times,* August 19, 2011.

[149] International Atomic Energy Agency. "Energy, Electricity and Nuclear Power Estimates for the Period up to 2050." Reference Data Series No. 1, International Atomic Energy Agency, Vienna, 2012; and Cala, Andres. "Russia Stands to Profit from Turn Away From Nuclear Power." *New York Times,* June 14, 2011.

[150] Müller-Kraenner, Sascha. *Energy Security: Re-Measuring the World.* London: Earthscan, 2008, quoting "World Energy Outlook 2006."

151 *The Economist.* "Glittering Towers In a War Zone." December 7, 2006.

152 Reuters. "Iran Offers India Oil Supply Plan for January." *The New York Times*, January 4, 2011.

153 *Ibid.*

154 Bagchi, Indrani. "India, Iran and Oman go under sea to build pipelines, change geopolitics." *The Times of India,* March 1, 2014.

155 Follath, Eric. "Natural Resources are Fuelling A New Cold War." *Der Spiegel,* August 18, 2006; and CRI. "China, Iran sign biggest oil & gas deal." *China Daily.* October 31, 2004. http://www.chinadaily.com.cn/english/doc/2004-10/31/content_387140.htm.

156 *Iran signs $3.2 bn natural gas deal with China.* March 16, 2009. http://www.seatrade-global.com/news/asia/Iran-signs-3632bn-natural-gas-deal-with-China.html.

157 Yep, Eric. "New Russia-China Deal Could Further Hit Natural-Gas Prices." *The Wall Street Journal*, November 10, 2014.

158 Rivera, Ray, and Ruhullah Khapalwak. "Afghans Strained by Shortages as Iran Tightens Flow of Fuel." *The New York Times*, January 9, 2011.

159 Myers, Steven Lee. "Memo From Moscow: Belarus Learns that Days of Wine and Roses are Over." *The New York Times*, January 12, 2007.

160 Kramer, Andrew E. "Russia Tightens Pressure On Ukraine with Rise in Natural Gas Price." *The New York Times*, April 1, 2014.

161 Unger, David J. "Kerry to Russia: Don't Use Energy as a Weapon in Ukraine Crisis." *The Christian Science Monitor*, April 2, 2014.

162 Kramer, Andrew E. "Gazprom threatens to cut off gas if Belarus rejects higher price." *The New York Times*, December 27, 2006.

163 Myers, Steven Lee. "Belarus and Russia Spar Over Crude Oil Cut Off." *The New York Times*, January 9, 2007.

164 Myers, Steven Lee. "Memo From Moscow: Putin's Assertive Diplomacy is Seldom Challenged." *The New York Times*, December 27, 2006.

165 Reuters. "Iran Hints of Reduction of Oil Sales Over Nuclear Dispute." *The New York Times*, October 2, 2005.

166 Forero, Juan. "Venezuela Cautions US It May Curtail Oil Exports." *The New York Times*, February 27, 2006.

167 Krauss, Clifford. "Split By Infighting, OPEC keeps a cap on oil." *The New York Times*, June 8, 2011.

168 International Atomic Energy Agency. "IAEA Annual Report 2013." *iaea.org*. International Atomic Energy Agency. 2014 at 2. http://www.iaea.org/sites/default/files/anrep2013_full_0.pdf.

169 Yeomans, Matthew. "Crude Politics – The United State, China and the race for oil security." *The Atlantic Monthly*, April 2005, at 49.

170 Connors, Will. "Nigeria Turns Over Disputed Land to Cameroon." *The New York Times*, August 14, 2008.

171 Associated Press. "Africa's Oil Comes with Big Downside." *New York Times*, August 28, 2005.

172 International Crisis Group. *Fuelling the Niger Delta Crisis.* Africa Report, Dakar & Brussels: International Crisis Group, September 28, 2006.

173 *Nigeria: Timeline of recent unrest in Niger Delta region.* UN Office for the Coordination of Humanitarian Affairs Integrated Regional Information Networks (IRIN). February 4, 2010. http://www.irinnews.org/report/88002/nigeria-timeline-of-recent-unrest-in-

niger-delta-region; and Shank, Michael, and Kate Edelen. "Cleaning Up Big Oil in Nigeria." *U.S. News and World Report*, July 31, 2014.

174 U.S. Energy Information Administration (EIA). "Sudan and South Sudan." *eia.gov*. September 3, 2014. http://www.eia.gov/countries/cab.cfm?fips=SU; and Gettleman, Jeffrey. "Sudan's Leader Reaches Out Ahead of Vote;" and *The New York Times*, January 4, 2011.

175 Kron, Josh. "South Sudan Reports Air Attacks by Sudan." *The New York Times*, April 23, 2012; and Kron, Josh. "South Sudan Says Sudan Strikes Again." *The New York Times*, April 24, 2012.

176 Kushkush, Isma'il. "Sudan Says Military Evicts South's Army From Oil Area." *The New York Times*, April 20, 2012.

177 Tabuchi, Hiroko. "Japan Scrambles Jets in Islands Dispute with China." *The New York Times*, December 13, 2012; and Perlez, Jane. "China and Japan, in Sign of a Thaw, Agree to Disagree on a Disputed Island Group;" and *The New York Times*, November 7, 2014.

178 *The Economist.* "China and Japan – Locked On." February 9, 2013; and BBC News. *How Uninhabited islands soured China-Japan ties.* British Broadcasting Company (BBC). November 9, 2014. http://www.bbc.com/news/world-asia-pacific-11341139.

179 U.S. Energy Information Administration (EIA). "East China Sea." *eia.gov*. September 17, 2014. http://www.eia.gov/countries/regions-topics.cfm?fips=ECS.

180 Ghosh, Palash. "Balochistan: Pakistan's 'Dirty War' In Its Poorest, Most Lawless, But Resource-Rich Province." *International Business Times*, September 14, 2013.

181 *The Economist.* "The Nagorno-Karabakh conflict: A Festering Sore." October 3, 2013.

[182] Grono, Nick. "Natural Resources and Conflict." Brussels: The International Crisis Group, May 31, 2006.

[183] Perlez, Jane. "Japan Makes Overture to China in Islands Dispute." *The New York Times*, January 22, 2013; and *The Economist*. "South-East Asia and China – All change at ASEAN." February 9, 2013.

[184] Müller-Kraenner, Sascha. *Energy Security: Re-Measuring the World*. London: Earthscan, 2008, at 149.

[185] Warrick, Joby, and Juliet Eilperin. "Warming Arctic Opens Way to Competition for Resources." *The Washington Post*, May 15, 2011.

[186] BBC News. "Canada Launches Mission to Map Arctic Seabed." British Broadcasting Company (BBC), August 8, 2014.

[187] Grono, Nick. "Addressing the links between conflicts and natural resources." Brussels, February 9, 2006.

[188] Soros, George. *Transparent Corruption*. DebtChannel. February 2003. https://www.globalpolicy.org/pmscs/30083.html.

[189] Palley, Thomas I. "Lifting the Natural Resource Curse." *Foreign Service Journal* (American Foreign Service Association) 80 (December 2003), at 54.

[190] Transparency International. *Oil and Gas*. http://www.transparency.org/topic/detail/oil_and_g as (accessed 2014).

[191] LaFraniere, Sharon. "In Oil-Rich Angola, Cholera Preys Upon Poorest." *The New York Times*, June 16, 2006; and Pendleton, Andrew, Judith Melby, Liz Stuart, Johnl Davison, and Sue Bishop. *Fuelling Poverty: Oil, War and Corruption*. Christian Aid, 2003.

[192] Duval-Smith, Alex. *Piped water projects offer health, opportunities to Angolan families*. U.N. Children's Fund

(UNICEF). January 2012, 25. http://www.unicef.org/wash/angola_61423.html.

193 U.S. Energy Information Administration (EIA). "Angola." *eia.gov.* February 5, 2014. http://www.eia.gov/countries/cab.cfm?fips=AO.

194 Polgreen, Lydia. "World Bank Reaches Pact with Chad over Use of Oil Profits." *The New York Times*, July 15, 2006; and Polgreen, Lydia, and Celia W. Dugger. "Chad's Oil Riches, Meant for Poor, Are Diverted;" and *The New York Times*, February 18, 2006.

195 Polgreen, Lydia. "World Bank Ends Effort to Help Chad Ease Poverty." *The New York Times*, September 10, 2008.

196 Palley, Thomas I. "Lifting the Natural Resource Curse." *Foreign Service Journal* (American Foreign Service Association) 80 (December 2003), at 54-61; and Transparency International. *Corruption by Country / Territory.* http://www.transparency.org/country (accessed 2013).

197 *US embassy cables: Kazakhstan's anti-corruption campaign.* The Guardian. November 29, 2010. http://www.theguardian.com/world/us-embassy-cables-documents/203528.

198 Interfax-Kazakhstan. *Experts say corruption in Kazakhstan becoming systemic.* Interfax-Kazakhstan. March 14, 2014. https://www.interfax.kz/index.php?lang=eng&int_id=expert_opinions&news_id=1437.

199 Kramer, Andrew E. "Russia Cashes In on Anxiety Over Supply of Middle East Oil." *The New York Times*, March 7, 2011.

200 Pendleton, Andrew, Judith Melby, Liz Stuart, Johnl Davison, and Sue Bishop. *Fuelling Poverty: Oil, War and Corruption.* Christian Aid, 2003, at 4.

201 Reuters. "Global Oil Producers Discuss Supply." *The New York Times*, November 19, 2005.

202 Caruso, Guy F. *More Transparency against the threat of price instability.* October 31, 2009. http://www.abo.net/oilportal/topic/view.do?contentId=2053054.

203 International Crisis Group. *Fuelling the Niger Delta Crisis.* Africa Report, Dakar & Brussels: International Crisis Group, September 28, 2006.

204 Vidal, John. "Niger Delta oil spills clean-up will take 30 years, says UN." *The Guardian*, August 4, 2011.

205 *Associated Press.* "Shell and Nigeria have failed on oil pollution clean-up, Amnesty says." August 4, 2014.

206 Nossiter, Adam. "China Finds Resistance to Oil Deals in Africa." *The New York Times*, September 17, 2013.

207 Rohter, Larry. "Vast Pipelines in Amazon Face Challenges Over Protecting Rights and Rivers." *The New York Times*, January 21, 2007; and Scott, Wallace. "Rain Forest for Sale: Demand for oil is squeezing the life out of one of the world's wildest places." *National Geographic*, January 2013, at 82.

208 Austen, Ian. "Oil Sands Industry in Canada Tied to Higher Carcinogen Level." *New York Times*, January 7, 2013.

209 *The Economist.* "Shale gas – Frack On." November 26, 2011.

210 *The Economist.* "The Economist Explains: How Safe is Fracking." August 19, 2013.

211 *The Economist.* "Natural gas in Oklahoma – will frack you." November 19, 2011.

212 *The Economist.* "Brazil's Offshore Oil/In Deep Waters." February 3, 2011.

213 Reuters. "Obama oil spill commission's final report blames disaster on cost-cutting by BP and partners." *The Telegraph*, January 5, 2011.

214 International Atomic Energy Agency. "IAEA Annual Report 2013." *iaea.org*. International Atomic Energy Agency. 2014, at 2. http://www.iaea.org/sites/default/files/anrep2013_full_0.pdf.

215 Fackler, Martin. "Surging Oil and Food Prices Threaten the World Economy, Finance Ministers Warn." *The New York Times*, June 15, 2008.

216 *The Economist.* "Petrol Prices – A Jump at the Pump." January 27, 2011.

217 *The Economist.* "The real trouble with oil." April 28, 2005.

218 United Nations General Assembly. "World Summit Outcome." *unrol.org*. October 24, 2005, at 31. http://www.unrol.org/doc.aspx?n=2005+World+Summit+Outcome.pdf.

219 *The Responsibility to Protect.* International Commission on Intervention and State Sovereignty, Ottawa: International Development Research Center, 2001, at 91.

220 U.N. Secretary General's High-level Panel on Threats, Challenges and Change. "A More Secure World: Our Shared Responsibility." United Nations Department of Public Information. December 2004, at para 203. https://www.un.org/en/peacebuilding/pdf/historical/hlp_more_secure_world.pdf.

221 Secretary General. *Secretary General, United Nations. In Larger Freedom: towards development, security and human rights for all. (A/59/2005). United Nations. 2005.* United Nations, 2005, at 35.

222 United Nations General Assembly. "World Summit Outcome." *unrol.org*. October 24, 2005, at 31.

http://www.unrol.org/doc.aspx?n=2005+World+Summit+Outcome.pdf.

223 Interview by Cyril Vanier. *World This Week* France 24. October 16, 2012.

224 McKirdy, Euan, Bryony Jones, and Susannah Cullinane. *Five Secessionist Movements That Could Learn From Scotland.* CNN. September 19, 2014. http://www.cnn.com/2014/09/17/world/scotland-five-other-separatist-movements/.

225 *The Economist.* "The Economist explains Catalonia's Independence Movement." October 14, 2014.

226 Erlanger, Steven, and Alan Cowell. "Scotland Rejects Independence from United Kingdom." *The New York Times*, September 18, 2014.

227 *The Economist.* "Cue for another Viking Raid." November 18, 2013.

228 Erlanger, Steven. "Britain Pledges More Self-Rule for Scots if They Reject Scottish Independence." *The New York Times*, September 7, 2014.

229 Erlanger, Steven, and Alan Cowell. "Scotland Rejects Independence from United Kingdom." *The New York Times*, September 18, 2014.

230 Herszenhorn, David M. "Crimea Votes to Seceded from Ukraine as Russian Troops Keep Watch." *The New York Times*, March 16, 2014.

231 BBC News. *South Sudan Profile.* BBC News Africa. August 6, 2014. http://www.bbc.com/news/world-africa-14069082.

About the Author

Sovaida Ma'ani Ewing writes and lectures in the area of global governance and international security. Prior to her current work as founding director of the Center for Peace and Global Governance, Ms. Ma'ani Ewing served as an Attorney-Advisor in the Legal Advisor's Office of the U.S. State Department. Born in East Africa and raised there and in the Middle East, she has also lived in the United Kingdom, where she earned an LLM in International Law and European Union law at Cambridge University and qualified as a barrister-at-law of England and Wales. She subsequently moved to the United States and qualified as an attorney-at-law there, practiced law at respected law firms in Washington, D.C., including her own, and taught as an adjunct professor of law at George Washington University's law school. Ms. Ma'ani Ewing has written several books, including *Collective Security Within Reach* (2008). She maintains a blog about solutions to current global issues at http://collectivesecurity.blogspot.com.

The Center for Peace and Global Governance

CPGG is a virtual think tank and online forum that pools and proposes principled solutions to pressing global problems through publications, podcasts, lectures, workshops and targeted consulting.

http://www.centerforpeaceandglobalgovernance.org

CPSIA information can be obtained at www.ICGtesting.com
Printed in the USA
LVOW04s2124160115

423153LV00033B/1644/P